W9-BST-022

THE GREAT WALL OF CHINA

AND THE

SALTON SEA

THE GREAT WALL OF CHINA
AND THE
SALTON SEA

....

Monuments, Missteps,
and the
Audacity of Ambition

Russell Rathbun

WILLIAM B. EERDMANS PUBLISHING COMPANY
GRAND RAPIDS, MICHIGAN

Flagstaff Public Library
Flagstaff, Arizona

Wm. B. Eerdmans Publishing Co.
2140 Oak Industrial Drive N.E., Grand Rapids, Michigan 49505
www.eerdmans.com

© 2017 Russell Rathbun
All rights reserved
Published 2017
Printed in the United States of America

23 22 21 20 19 18 17   1 2 3 4 5 6 7

ISBN 978-0-8028-7365-1

Library of Congress Cataloging-in-Publication Data

Names: Rathbun, Russell, author.
Title: The Great Wall of China and the Salton Sea : monuments, missteps, and
    the audacity of ambition / Russell Rathbun.
Description: Grand Rapids : Eerdmans Publishing Co., 2017.
Identifiers: LCCN 2016035930 | ISBN 9780802873651 (cloth : alk. paper)
Subjects: LCSH: Rathbun, Russell—Travel. | Christian biography. |
    Spirituality—Christianity. | Spiritual life—Christianity.
Classification: LCC BR1725.R3355 A3 2017 | DDC 270.092 [B] —dc23
    LC record available at https://lccn.loc.gov/2016035930

1234

For Betty Lee Rathbun and Franklin Lee Webb,

my mom and my grandpa

Contents

Foreword

When Russell told me that he was writing about ambition in *The Great Wall of China and the Salton Sea*, I was thrilled—but also maybe a little nervous. I've been thinking about ambition a lot recently, perhaps because I have a personal confusion about it. There's this weird way in which I never really *tried* to be a writer or a speaker or a public persona—I've just responded to things that were put in front of me.

The way I am thinking about it, ambition is having a certain idea I like to have of myself, or my church, or my organization—like I should be published, or wouldn't it feel amazing to have my church be seen as open and affirming, or maybe if my organization was more multicultural, people would admire it. And when there's a distance between where I am and where that idea is manifested, then ambition is trying to figure out what I am going to do to cross that distance.

Ambition is something I have this odd relationship with. I know I *have* ambition because, for instance, if Oprah Winfrey's people called and said, "We want you to be part of this 'Super Soul Sunday,'" I would be like, "Awesome—yes!"

But what I've been wondering is what's the difference between call and ambition, and when do we confuse the two? This is the question I keep coming back to.

There are some truly great aspects to human ambition.

Ambition drives us to make beautiful things. Like the polio vaccine. Jonas Salk. That was ambition, right? But there is always a way in which the monumental results that benefit the world are also an accidental by-product of our own ego. Or our inflated ego results from our realized ambition. It is creation and it is destruction at the same time. The fact that so many of the good things have been wrought through an ambition to be someone important or to be remembered, though a self-serving motive, doesn't negate the value they bring to the world. Even for Jonas Salk, his motivation could have been, "I'm going to do something really important. I'm going to be remembered." But yet, the effect was something really beautiful, glorious, healing, and life-giving to so many people.

There is simply no purity to be had in the world. Perhaps this is why I think we should be talking more honestly about the ambiguity of ambition, rather than pretending altruism is possible.

If there were no ambition, some great things wouldn't exist. Still, that doesn't mean that ambition is in some way pure. In his book Russell talks about the conflicting impulses of ambition in ways that are sometimes a little dark and sometimes a little hilarious.

Thirteen years ago, when I met Russell, I immediately felt like, "Oh, thank God, I'm not the only one." I had no idea that it was possible to love Jesus and maybe even love the church, and at the same time have a sort of pleasingly low anthropology and a sort of cutting cynicism. This particular combination you just don't often see in our fellows.

So when I met Russell, I immediately felt, "Oh, I might be part of a tribe I didn't know existed." Discovering Russell and his church, House of Mercy, inspired my thinking that maybe it would be worth it to start a church. Maybe it's possible to start a church I'd actually want to show up to.

Russell is not afraid of the Bible, and because of that, there is no way to approach it that is off-limits for him; clearly he has the incredibly high regard for the text that you only witness in someone not afraid of the text. As a result Russell finds quirky, surprising, and completely unique interpretations of the text that shed light and give clarity to what it means to be a human living in the twenty-first century in a world spinning out of control.

The way he plays with the Flood and the Tower of Babel stories from Genesis in this book is brilliant. I myself am more prone to say, "These are projections of what ancient people thought God must be like, so that people explained natural phenomena like a flood or an earthquake by saying, 'This happened, and so this must be God causing it. It must be God's nature.'" But today we know that can't really be what God is like, right?

But Russell says, "No, no, no—that's definitely God's personality according to the narrative in this biblical story, so let's deal with that. Let's figure out where to find the mercy starting from there." He is not going to apologize because God might come off like kind of an asshole sometimes. So many people treat God like their alcoholic father, you know? They have to apologize for him—to make a lot of excuses for him—saying, "But when he's sober, he's so nice." But Russell just jumps into the text, with a line like, "Well, he did just kill nearly every living being in this flood." He is simply unafraid.

Russell thinks the Bible is strong enough to hold up to

any approach. That, to me, is what having a high regard for Scripture looks like. He trusts the tradition and the Spirit embedded in these stories. And as readers of *The Great Wall of China and the Salton Sea,* you can trust that this book will change the way you understand these stories in history, and in the Bible, and most importantly, in the story we're living now.

NADIA BOLZ-WEBER

Acknowledgments

This book did not start out as the obsession with its subject matter that has increasingly occupied me for almost the last five years, and looks to be with me for at least another five, but I know whom to thank for it ending up this way. Lil Copan helped spark the original concept and made it better every step of the way. The germ of the book, as well as many of its themes, comes from an ongoing conversation with my colleague Rev. Debbie Blue. Erin Bowley has read and helped fix every incarnation of every chapter. And the book benefited from the mad skills of Mary Hietbrink, as well as Laura Bardolph Hubers and Rachel Bomberger, at Eerdmans.

I am indebted to the work of James Alison and Avivah Gottlieb Zornberg, my theological God Parents. If the book seems reminiscent of Sarah Vowell, that's because when I grow up, I want to be like her. In my research I have relied heavily on *The Salton Sea: Yesterday and Today* by Mildred de Stanley, *Plagues and Pleasures on the Salton Sea* by Chris Metzler and Jeff Springer, *The First Thirty Years* by Otis B. Tout, *Greetings from the Salton Sea: Folly and Intervention in the Southern California Landscape, 1905-2005* by Kim Stringfellow, and Al Kalin. I am grateful for interviews, anecdotes, and advice from Connie Barrington of the Imperial County Free Library, Eric Garcia, Frank J. Salazar III and the Imperial Valley Desert Museum, The Salton Sea History Museum, Geneva and Dean Davidsen, Norm Wuytens, and Leanne Rutherford and the Imperial County Historical Society Pioneers' Park Museum. I am also grateful for the hospitality of Ben Baker and Jodi Montgomery, and their memories of Luther Grass and Amos Jones. I also want to thank Greg Daniels, Nadia Bolz-Weber, Thad Dahlberg, Forest Lewis, Jonathan Haynes, my attorney John Soshnik, and Jeff and the MCTC Nursing Program. My thanks also go to Luke Finsaas at *Revolver*, who first published *Lament*, the inspiring folks at House of Mercy, and Erin Bowley and Jeremy Szopinski for material, moral, and hip-hop support.

Finally, my deepest thanks go to my family—Bob and Betty Rathbun, Kim Rathbun, Pam and Mike Wurtz, Matt and Cyndi Rathbun, Jackie and Ralph DiMeglio—and especially to Jeanne, Joe, and Maria, whose real sacrifice and love make everything possible.

And of course my brother Mike.

Introduction

*There are only two man-made objects you can see from
outer space. One is the Great Wall of China, and the
other is the Salton Sea. One is the result of the work of
hundreds of thousands of laborers over two thousand
years, and the other is the result of a gigantic mistake.*

This book is born out of these three sentences loitering
in my brain for the last twenty-something years and
an unsettled feeling about who I really am—in relationship
to God, other people, history, and the created world—you
know, the little questions.

Those lines are statement and poem and koan. And
they are also the opening lines of a story about the inherent human impulse and/or original commandment of God
to spread out, build up, occupy, make, and establish through
histories grand and mundane. Sometimes, shining and sub-
lime, this is a continuation of God's unfolding creation. At
other times it is the delusional pursuit of empire's repressed
desire to cuckold the Creator—which always seems to get
kind of ugly. And catastrophic. And death-y.

Usually there is no clear initial intention on the part of
people to get catastrophic and death-y—many times we're
too far down the road before we realize we took the wrong

turn. Maybe this book is an attempt to get some perspective, to give ourselves a chance to see things up close and from a vast distance.

> *There are only two man-made objects you can see from outer space. One is the Great Wall of China, and the other is the Salton Sea. One is the result of the work of hundreds of thousands of laborers over two thousand years, and the other is the result of a gigantic mistake.*

In between sessions at a conference in Minneapolis, my editor asked me, "Is there an idea you want to know more about, research and write about? Not some subject that you care about and have already come to some conclusions about— but something that baffles you, that you suspect might be important."

"Alienation." I had the word on the edge of my teeth before she finished the question. I had been wondering for a while about the idea of alienation and the search for its cause and cure that was of such interest to theologians, psychologists, philosophers, and sociologists in the late nineteenth and early twentieth centuries, and that was popularized in the 1960s and 1970s. People were trying to *find themselves* and *search for themselves*, wanting to know who they were in connection to God, others, and the created world.

Walker Percy was a mid-twentieth-century Southern, Catholic writer of novels and nonfiction who explored alienation. In his satiric *Lost in the Cosmos: The Last Self-Help Book* he asks, "Why is it possible to learn more in ten minutes about the Crab Nebula in Taurus, which is 6,000 light years away, than you presently know about yourself, even though you've been stuck with yourself all your life?" Part of the impetus for wanting to write this book came out of thinking about Percy's exploration of the "alienation of modern man."

I wonder: In what ways has technology re-formed the self in the twenty-first century, and what are the effects of mediated connections on who we are and why we are? Do our digital lives provide us with an illusion that numbs or masks our desire for real connection to God, others, and the created world? The dominance of digitally mediated interactions is barely over a decade old. (Facebook was founded in 2004, Twitter in 2006.) We're only beginning to understand the spiritual and cultural effects. The previous wave of interest in alienation was sparked as people sought to find meaning in the wake of the Industrial Revolution. As a result of the Digital Revolution, I suspect that we are beginning to see a similar unmooring.

There are only two man-made objects you can see from outer space. One is the Great Wall of China, and the other is the Salton Sea. One is the result of the work of hundreds of thousands of laborers over two thousand years, and the other is the result of a gigantic mistake.

The ancient rabbis say that the study of Torah releases God's mercy into the world. In the rabbinic biblical interpretive tradition of Midrash, the rabbis study the biblical texts deeply, telling stories, drawing conclusions, making arguments, comparisons, proclamations—contradicting one, supporting another, quibbling, and often seeming to make no earthly sense—all in an attempt to get a glimpse of the word of God, which may be almost completely unknowable.

xix

This investigation, this contemplative narrative is midrashic in structure. I tell stories about the Great Wall of China and the Salton Sea, about the Tower of Babel and the Great Flood, about Madame Mao and her Gang of Four, about my Grandpa Webb—his Union Study Bible and his Thirty-Aught-Six Springfield rifle. I tell all these stories in an attempt to get a glimpse of what it might mean to be me here, now—in relationship to God, other people, history, and the created world—to acknowledge my participation in the continuation of creation and my complicity in the dull march of empire.

I have a notion that my search, unlike that of previous generations, is not a search for the self and its place in the universe. It may have more to do with being discovered, noticed. Not crossing the Great Plains into uncharted land or taking one giant leap on the moon for mankind and planting a flag, but stumbling in the desert, looking up into the sun, one hand shielding my eyes and the other waving, saying, "Hey, I'm here. Can you see me?"

CHAPTER 1

The Monumental and the Missteps . . .
Irrigating the Desert . . .
The Deluge . . .
A Very Big Beaver Dam . . .
Creation as Separation . . .
Riffing on the Rabbis . . .
Longing to Catch a Glimpse of God . . .

There are only two man-made objects you can see from outer space. One is the Great Wall of China, and the other is the Salton Sea. One is the result of the work of hundreds of thousands of laborers over two thousand years, and the other is the result of a gigantic mistake.

From space it's hard to tell the monumental from the missteps. Even down here on earth it's not that easy. We have been building things and making stuff since we stumbled out of Paradise. Our hard-working forebears built shelters, walls, tribes, and empires; they made roads, borders, and grand structures. And some pretty big messes.

All that eagerness to *go forth and establish* makes it hard to stop and consider how a venture might end up. With the benefit of history and its interpreters, we should have better insight into what makes the difference between creating a jewel in our crown and constructing a bewildering catastrophe that threatens our existence.

As early as the seventh century BCE, Chinese rulers began building the wall. These early sections of it were built using the rammed-earth method, which is simple but hard. Basically it involves piling a load of dirt in a stone form, dampening it with water, adding a little lime or animal blood (really, animal blood) as a binder, and then ramming it down until it's half its original size—and then doing that again and again until the wall is tall enough to please whichever ruler is calling the shots.

The greatest Great Wall-building ruler was Qin Shi Huangdi. At age thirteen he inherited the throne of the western Chinese kingdom of Qin. The newly crowned teenager claimed to have a vision that he would bring power and glory to the name of Qin—more greatness then anyone, ever—and he would unite all of the warring kingdoms of China into one great country, the greatest country ever. Teenagers tend towards self-centered grandiosity, and if you're a teenage king, bragging that you're going to be the best king in the whole world and beat up all the other kings and take all their kingdoms and turn them into one super-big country seems like the kind of outrageous claim you might make. But Qin Shi Huangdi actually did it.

It took twenty-five years, but Qin defeated the other six major kingdoms and for the first time unified China. His conquest, however, was about more than just individual power or bringing glory to his tribe. In his vision he flew high into the sky and, looking down, saw all the peoples of the warring kingdoms come together. As if he was looking at an animated map, he saw the borders of the seven kingdoms moving and merging together to form one border encompassing them all. For more than 250 years the kingdoms had been at war over territorial disputes, draining their wealth and limiting their prosperity. Qin saw that, as one great state under his flag, China and her people could prosper. He could build something the world had never seen.

After declaring himself China's first emperor (literally, what *Qin Shi Huangdi* means), he became obsessed with unity at every level. He combined the seven different forms of the written language into one official version. He standardized weights and measurements and wrote laws dictating the one right way to do everything, whether you were killing a pigeon, buying rice, or losing your virginity. He made the writers of Leviticus look like slackers. To encourage trade and cultural exchange between the former states, he built a network of roads connecting every part of the new empire and called for massive building projects employing millions of peasants. He wanted his people to be happy and united, insisting that everything should be the same everywhere.

And to protect his glorious unified empire, he embarked on the largest public-works program the world would ever know. In his vision, Qin not only saw the warring kingdoms become one, but saw China's future secured by a great wall traversing its entire northern border and shielding it from outside invaders.

Inspired, Qin linked together existing walls built by the feudal kings and extended the Great Wall from several hundred miles to over three thousand miles, completing the monumental task in just fifteen years—and then he died.

Qin's Great Wall was an unprecedented feat of engineering and imperial vision. But as a barrier to keep out the northern hordes, it was less successful. As impressive as the Great Wall of China continues to be as an immense man-made structure, it never worked very well as an actual wall. There weren't enough soldiers in China to man the wall, and the relatively few guards on lookout were easily bribed. And, once mounted, the wide, smooth, stone top of the wall served as a sort of East-West highway that allowed invaders to make pretty good time.

Still, subsequent dynasties continued the construction. Over two thousand years of building, more than a million laborers worked on the wall. The majority of the wall surviving today was built during the Ming dynasty, from the fourteenth to the seventeenth centuries. Archaeological surveys estimate it to be anywhere from five thousand to thirteen thousand miles long, running along high mountain ridges, passing through deserts, and finally extending into the sea.

SIX THOUSAND MILES away and four hundred years after the Ming dynasty came the Salton Sea, the other man-made object you can see from outer space. A prominent feature of the California desert, it's an inland sea fifteen miles wide and thirty-five miles long, created by accident.

When the forces of manifest destiny ran up against the Pacific Ocean, they started looking around for something more to do. They looked back over their shoulders and saw the Colorado Desert. The desert spreads out from the mountains east of San Diego to the Colorado River, and from Palm Springs to the Mexican border. In 1896 a group of enterprising land developers saw all that cheap, un-arable land and the mighty Colorado River flowing uselessly into the ocean—and they had an idea.

They could divert the river into a series of canals, irrigating the desert and turning it into productive farmland. The climate could produce four harvests a year, creating the need for workers and houses and towns, for all kinds of infrastructure—and these men of vision, these men of destiny could build and sell it all. What could go wrong?

Forming the California Development Company, they built the canals to divert the Colorado River. Their ambitious work progressed, and by 1900, they formed the Imperial Land Company to sell land to all the farmers and ranchers the irrigated desert would attract. They laid out five town sites, prepared thousands of acres for farming and ranching, and then put up the For Sale signs.

They renamed the desert the Imperial Valley to make it sound lush, attractive, and to, you know, downplay the whole desert thing. Like Qin Shi Huangdi, they were creating something the world had never seen before. Theirs was an empire in the desert. Through the sheer force of their own will and moxie, they would make water stream through the desert and transform it into a green and profitable garden.

In short, these men were trying to create something out of what looked to them like almost nothing, a quasi *ex nihilo*, where they stepped in to play God's role.

The newly christened Imperial Valley was located in the Salton Sink, a geological area 234 feet below sea level. The depression is right on top of the San Andreas Fault—in an active tectonic pull-apart zone—which means that the "sink" part of the Salton Sink is caused by the seismic activity actually pulling the earth's crust apart. It probably sounds worse than it is.

And lest you think these men of vision were merely cynical, environment-hating capitalists, remember that the calendar was still turning over from the nineteenth century to the twentieth, and that they had no idea that a desert was a fully functioning and necessary ecosystem—they just thought it was dirt. Besides, they had God on their side. Not only were they high on the rhetoric of manifest destiny, which drove men forward with the velocity of meth-heads; their vision had precedents. Isaiah, the greatest Old Testament prophet, seemed to speak to them.

At the time, the book *Streams in the Desert* was the most popular Christian devotional. Written by Lettie B. Cowman, who published under the name Mrs. Charles E. Cowman, *Streams in the Desert* took its name from Isaiah 35:6: ". . . For waters shall break forth in the wilderness, and streams in the desert." So these men weren't just trying to make a buck; they were up to something of biblical proportions. But their interpretation was flawed: Isaiah's vision of streams in the desert was a metaphor for God pouring sustenance into the barren souls of God's children, not an engineering proposal.

Nevertheless, the dream of development continued. The company's chief engineer, R. C. Rookwood, had a grand vision: to turn the barren land of the Salton Sink into the greatest irrigation project the world had ever seen. Once the network of small canals and individual farm plots was created, he put his men to work on the All-American Canal. This eighty-mile-long conduit would carry waters from the diverted Colorado River to Imperial Valley, where the subduing of the desert would begin.[1]

By 1905 the work was complete, and a considerable

---

1. Robert L. Sperry, "When the Imperial Valley Fought for Its Life," *The Journal of San Diego History* 21:1 (1975).

number of farmers and ranchers had already moved into the area—just waiting on the water to start their soil tilling, beef growing, and general prospering on the land. A date was set to throw the switch and open the floodgates that would send the Colorado River leaping into the All-American Canal. A dais was built. Dignitaries were invited.

On the appointed day, the governors of California and Arizona were there, as was the governor of the Mexican state of Baja California. Even President Teddy Roosevelt attended. A band played, speeches were given, and then the floodgates were opened.

The Colorado rushed into the canal, its roiling waters charging toward Imperial Valley. Now, this was the Colorado River, the river that carved the Grand Canyon, the river now swollen from a very snowy winter in the Rockies. Had the engineer failed to take these factors into account, or was this a much graver miscalculation? What happened next suggests the latter.

When the water reached the big bend in the canal meant to divert the water south, the river didn't stop. It didn't bend. It didn't turn. It smashed through the side of the All-American Canal and into the desert.

Seeking the lowest point, as any water will, the deluge flooded to the lowest point in the Salton Sink, over 200 feet below sea level, and started filling up the desert. God may have been speaking to the men of the Imperial Land Company through Isaiah, but they may have failed to read the whole verse. Sure, it says there will be streams in the desert, nurture for parched souls. But the line before reads "waters shall break forth in the wilderness." And indeed they did. It seems that Isaiah's prophecy covered both possibilities.

The rushing water quickly carved a new bed in the dry soil straight to the center of the Salton Sink. The engineers of the California Development Company tried every possible method to close the break and get the river back on track, but everything they did easily washed away. The Southern Pacific Railroad finally got involved: with miles of their main line through Imperial Valley already underwater, they didn't want to lose any more. They built tracks up to the edge of the breach and filled boxcars with sand and ran them off the end, eventually closing the gap and successfully diverting the river into the All-American Canal. By that time it was 1907. The Colorado River had been filling up the desert for two years, creating a sea fifteen miles wide, thirty-five miles long, and eighty feet deep.

Even a body of water that big would eventually evaporate in the desert, but the agricultural run-off from the irrigated land found its way to the Salton Sea, continually feeding it Colorado River water—although now it was mixed with chemical fertilizers and animal feces.

My freshman year of college, my mom and dad and younger sister and brother moved to Brawley, one of the original five towns laid out by the Imperial Land Company. I lived there on a two-year hiatus from college—I had to quit and pay off my tuition bill before I could start up again.

I grew up in the city, love public transportation, and get a little scared at night when I'm camping in the wilderness. Imperial Valley was like no place I even had a reference for. The built environment barely made a mark on the landscape. Every road, shed, or taco stand started losing its battle with the elements the moment it was built. There was scorching sun, buckling heat, torrid wind, baked earth, and every other built and living thing trying to survive them.

I don't remember who first told me the Salton Sea creation story because I heard it so many times when I was living in Imperial Valley. Every time, I thought, *Is there any way to live through a mistake that catastrophic? Do you try to disappear, hope your shame is diluted in the flood, or pray that somehow, somewhere else on the planet, someone else is screwing up more flamboyantly than you?*

What is it like to have such grand ambition and fail on such a grand scale? These men thought they were making their mark on the world. They would be remembered for the greatness of their achievement, harnessing Mother Nature and bending her will for the good of humanity. And they did leave a mark on the earth. Fifteen miles wide, thirty-five miles long, and eighty feet deep.

As I said, I don't remember if I first heard the story from Luther Grass or Amos Jones or Frank Slaughter's dad, but whoever told it, it nearly always started the same way: *There are only two man-made objects you can see from outer space. One is the Great Wall of China, and the other is the Salton Sea.*

Sometimes that was all that was said. "Really?" I would respond. "That's amazing." Other times I got the whole story. Every telling was a little different, more or less detail, more or less drama, depending on the storyteller.

Luther Grass was Cherokee. I don't remember the story of how he ended up in Imperial Valley, but there weren't a lot of Cherokee in Brawley. He was a retired chemist for the Imperial Irrigation District. One time we were talking after church about school or something, and I told him I had never taken a chemistry class because it just didn't seem like it would be very interesting. (I know—but I was only twenty-four. I hope my remark wasn't as rude or arrogant as it sounds now.) Luther just smiled and said he didn't know why I wouldn't be interested in the building blocks of every living thing. He was the most understated, eloquent storyteller.

Amos Jones, the retired Brawley fire chief, had been a bad boy in the forties, driving his motorcycle through the desert at a hundred miles an hour. He showed me how to kick a latched chain-link fence gate in the right spot so it would fly open and you wouldn't even have to slow down if you were running to rescue someone or put out a fire. He had me practice on the gate behind the church. Amos was gregarious and charming. When he told the story, he filled it with a lot of detail and a lot of action.

No matter who told the story, a glint of pride shined behind the tale—even though it was a tale of incredible hubris and a colossal natural disaster. Was it purely hometown pride, the kind of pride you would show if you could say, "Judy Garland's uncle used to live around here," or was it something about the association with the scale of the mistake? A dark pride.

Maybe for folks in the desert, the association with the Great Wall of China gives the Salton Sea a kind of exotic flavor or the impression that it's a sort of runner-up to one of the Seven Wonders of the World.

Maybe it's just the fact that there are only two man-made objects you can see from outer space. One is the Great Wall of China, and the other is the Salton Sea. *You can see them from outer space.* And maybe every retelling of the tale is like an inching ever closer to the object, so if anyone up there is looking down, they'll notice the teller, notice *me* standing next to it. Maybe it's not pride, dark or otherwise. Maybe it's an unconscious desire to be seen, to be connected to something big enough to matter.

WHILE THE STORY says that you can only see two man-made objects from outer space, there are claims for many more. There are the Palm Islands in Dubai, a forty-five-square-mile man-made archipelago, built in the shape of a palm tree. A company from the Netherlands was hired for the construction. The Dutch know a lot about building in the sea. After the North Sea flooded the coastal areas in 1953, killing more than 1,800 people, they built a higher, artificial coastline to keep the water at bay—a coastline, it is said, that can be seen from outer space. Then there's the Pentagon, the largest office building in the world, as well as the People's House in Bucharest, the second-largest office building in the world. Both are said to be visible from outer space—though probably not at the same time. And the lights of Las Vegas claim to be visible from outer space—though they're not technically one object, and, in truth, the claims are probably made on their behalf.

A left-leaning political website reports that the gap between the rich and the poor can be seen from outer space. Others say the BP oil spill, algae blooms, sewage, and the garbage patch, that floating island of plastic the size of Texas in the North Pacific Gyre, can be seen from outer space. On a cheerier note, fans of what is described as "a very big beaver dam" in Canada claim that, believe it or not, the dam can be seen from outer space. I think "beaver made" counts.

I really want to believe that a bunch of Canadian beavers

made a dam that big. And I like to imagine an astronaut glancing out the window of the space shuttle and shouting to his astronaut pals, "Look at the size of that beaver dam!" But it does raise an interesting question: Are people actually seeing these things from outer space? Or is it more likely that they *think* they can—"These lights are so bright I bet you could see them from outer space!" In the entire history of the world, only 517 people have ever been in a position to make the claim. Do they keep a running list? The first person to claim that the Great Wall of China could be seen from outer space was the Englishman William Stukeley—in 1754.

WITH ALL THIS looking down on or at other things and people, you have to be located in a position to look *from*. You have to be a distinct you. According to classic psychoanalytic theory, the realization of the other gives birth to the self.

When you notice someone noticing you, you realize you exist. Being noticed by the other/another confirms your self's existence and sparks meaning. This first happens when a baby becomes aware of their mother as a separate being. An incredible other being.

Claiming that something can be seen from outer space— telling someone about the exaggerated enormity of the Palm Islands of Dubai or the Canadian beaver dam—isn't about the object; it's about the teller, about the say-er. When William Stukeley returned from China and sat down with his friend Isaac Newton at the Royal Society Club, he said, "Sir Isaac, buddy, you're not going to believe it! This wall is so big, it can be seen from outer space." Stukeley wasn't talking about the size of the wall; he was trying to convince Newton of *his* size, of *his* importance. In telling the story, he was inching closer to the wall, posing with it in a picture, hoping Newton would see the two together and say, "My, you two certainly are impressive!" Although Newton, having invented the first reflecting telescope, probably saw through the outer-space boast.

STUKELEY CLAIMED THAT the Great Wall of China could be seen from outer space two hundred years before Soviet cosmonaut Yuri Gagarin was the first human being to actually look at the earth from space. But the whole idea of looking down on the earth from the heavens is much older. Much, much older, since right before time started.

Page one (after you get past the lists of abbreviations and table of contents and translation notes) of the Bible narrates creation from above. "In the beginning, God created the heavens and the earth. The earth was without form and void, and darkness was over the face of the deep. And the Spirit of God was hovering over the face of the waters."[2]

The very first thing God does is to make it possible to see something from outer space. God creates the heavens and the earth and then hovers above the earth and sees that it is good. Is good-ness the first thing that could ever be seen from outer space? The rest of the first chapter narrates the unfolding of creation from that perspective, from above, from God's perspective. At this point in the story, that's the only perspective there is.

The writers of Genesis tell us that the very first thing God does is to make one thing or no thing into two things—

---

2. Genesis 1:1–2, in *Holy Bible: English Standard Version*, vol. 1 (Wheaton, Ill.: Crossway Bibles, 2001).

the heavens and the earth. Now one can be seen from the other. God creates a place for God's creation to be, to belong, and another place that God's creation can gaze up into, searching for a glimpse of God.

Perspective—viewing, regarding, considering, contemplating—is only possible with distance. And distance requires separation. The ancient rabbis describe the act of creation as the act of separation. For six days creation continues, seen from God's perspective. He separates the heavens and the earth, separates the light from the darkness, the upper waters from the lower waters, the sea from the dry land, and the moon from the sun. God locates one here and the other there, creating a relationship full of interaction, dependence, longing, tension, and meaning.

Avivah Gottlieb Zornberg is an original thinker and writer about the biblical text. She has been studying Torah since she was a little girl in Scotland. She began reading Torah with her father, a prominent rabbi in Glasgow. With a Ph.D. in literature from Oxford University, she brings deep knowledge of the rabbinic tradition—as well as literary criticism, Lacanian psychology, poetry, Shakespeare, sociology, and all kinds of diverse and interesting sources—to her readings of the biblical texts. Like the ancient rabbis, she finds truths in the cracks and fissures of the holy writ, truths about God and grace and the human condition—and me. I feel like she understands something that I'm trying to understand about what it means to be a person existing in the world, about alienation, location, and reconciliation, about how hard and joyful and contentious and interesting it is to be human. How hard it is to find real connections to God, other people, and the created world. How hard it is to live life in the present without anxiety about the future or regret about the past.

Zornberg, riffing on the rabbis, writes that the act of creation as separation continues through Adam and Eve's expulsion from Paradise—that they are not actually, fully human until they're separated from complete intimacy with God and each other. Before they're sent out of the Garden, they are one with God and each other, a sort of unity of psyche. They are the infants who don't know where they end and their mother begins, and, like infants, they have no self-awareness. They cannot see each other, cannot long for or desire each other because there is no distance between them.

In the midrash the ancient rabbis tell a story about God's creation of Adam, saying that God formed him from the dust and then took him, captivated him with beautiful words, and seduced him into the Garden. Whispered in Adam's ear, perhaps, the meaning of life or the mystery of life. These words of seduction are buried deep in Adam's unconscious. When God separates Adam and Eve from the Garden and they are able to see each other for the first time, when their primal single-mindedness—one with God, one with each other—gives way to the separate minds of man, woman, and God, they experience desire for the first time. The secret words of seduction buried in the unconscious move them to desire reunion, but that kind of unity isn't possible outside of Paradise. They must live in time, time between what they want and need and the possibility of getting it.

This knowledge that one is separate from God and others and, in the oddest way, from one's self—this makes anguish and anxiety possible, but it also makes love and joy possible. On the other side of the gate, Adam remembers that he once fully knew God and Eve and was himself fully known. And he wants to get back there.[3]

The story in Genesis is as much a midrash on the meaning of life as it is the beginning of a tall tale. As much a parable about the mystery of what it means to be human as it is an odd origin story.

THERE ARE ONLY two man-made objects you can see from outer space. One is the Great Wall of China, and the other is the Salton Sea. One is the result of the work of hundreds of thousands of laborers over two thousand years, and the other is the result of a gigantic mistake.

Whether mistake or marvel, both objects are the result of striving, longing to do something monumental, something unprecedented to achieve greatness, wealth, power, recognition. Or maybe both are the acts of men compelled by the unconscious desire simply to be visible from outer space. Do those words God whispered into Adam's ear, meaning or mystery, live in everyone's unconscious? Are we all connected by these secret words? And what did God say?

Adam himself is standing on top of the Great Wall of China, next to the Salton Sea, right beside Amos Jones and William Stukeley and me. We're all looking up, longing to catch a glimpse of God looking down on us.

---

3. Avivah Gottlieb Zornberg, *The Beginning of Desire: Reflections on Genesis* (New York: Image Books, 1996).

I am at my Grandma and Grandpa Webb's house alone, walking from room to room, looking at paintings and photographs, figurines on doilies, things that have been there since I was a little kid. When I walk into their bedroom, a wall suddenly becomes a door. I put my hand on the knob, turn it slowly, and look in. I feel a dull exhilaration, a shadowed expectation. When I step in, I think I see some kind of light—but the dream ends there.

The dream was so real that I wondered if there was any way there could be a room in my grandma and grandpa's house that I had missed all my life, never noticed. I wanted there to be.

Apparently the "finding a new room" dream is common. I had this one during my first year of college. In dream analysis, the interpretation of the new-room dream suggests opening up a new part of yourself, a readiness to deal with a part of yourself that you've hidden, or a search for something new in your life. For me, it felt like a place I wanted to get back to, a place I had known once. It was far away, but I longed to pull it closer, so I could see it all.

Years after my Grandpa Webb died, my mom was going through his papers before selling the house. She found the deed to a lot in a resort development in Salton City, along with a brochure titled "Welcome to the Hottest Real Estate Development in the History of the Southern California Desert." Apparently my grandpa had gone on a free sales trip in the early sixties to the Salton Sea, and he had actually bought something.

This was a man who didn't spend money easily. He would do anything, as he often said, to save a scrap of pipe or a length of rope. He repainted his 1965 Ford F150 every couple of years with leftover house paint and a broom. When he cooked oatmeal every morning, he turned the gas burner off before it was done cooking and "let it coast." So it was hard for me to believe that he had bought vacation property in a resort development in a faraway desert.

Well, my mom explained, he hadn't bought the actual lot. He had purchased the rights to buy a lot in the resort development at some future, distant date. A right it wasn't clear he had ever exercised. I didn't know my grandpa had ever been to the Salton Sea, let alone owned rights to buy Salton Sea property.

EVEN THOUGH I moved away from Imperial Valley to finish college twenty years ago, the Salton Sea story has stayed with me, like feeling the cavity of a missing tooth with my tongue or remembering a book I read all day in bed when I stayed home sick from school. *There are only two man-made objects you can see from outer space. One is the Great Wall of China, and the other is the Salton Sea.* I had heard and told that story so often, but I had never been to the actual sea. I had sped by it countless times on Highway 86, driving between Brawley and Los Angeles, but I had never pulled off the main road to drive into the towns along the edge of the sea.

After my mom told me about my grandpa's purchase agreement, I couldn't help thinking that, because it was so unlike anything he'd do, it might mean something. I imagined him sitting at the kitchen table at night, looking over that agreement and that brochure, wondering if the dream was possible, longing for a distant self, one more like who he really was—not a kid the Depression had drained of every possibility but hard work and doing without. Out in the distance, in the future, he might be able to see himself as the owner of a resort home, playing with his daughters in the pool, his wife waving to him from the patio.

This wasn't a towering dream like the one Qin Shi Huangdi had, seeing the warring kingdoms united within a great wall stretching thirteen thousand miles. It wasn't an expansive vision like the California Development Company's brainstorm to bend an ancient, powerful river to its will in order to turn a barren desert into a garden paradise. But my grandpa's dream might have come from the same unconscious desire. To build something that mattered, that might pull him closer to the unknown promise of those whispered words. To build something up, or out and across, or to burrow down into, to plant himself and his family in a place that felt like home—where they had all once belonged, where the soil was part of him and not blowing away.

Imagining that Grandpa Webb might have believed he could find a different self in the distant desert increased my desire to go to the Salton Sea. I was longing for a past, a possibility, a place that I know was never there, but always might be there. You can spot the Salton Sea from outer space, but I had barely glimpsed it from my car window.

And now that I had discovered that I practically had roots there—family history, inheritance, contingent birthright—I wanted to see it close up.

I called my brother Mike and asked him if he wanted to help me find Grandpa's plot of land on the Salton Sea. When he said yes, I jumped in my car and drove the 1,740 miles from St. Paul, Minnesota, to Portland, Oregon, and picked him up. Then we drove the 1,162 miles to the Salton Sea.

"It is hard to believe that this land of sparkling turquoise blue, of marinas and luxury homes, was an uninhabited desert wasteland only a little more that seventy years ago. Those times are so strange and so far removed from our way of life, that they seem unbelievable."[1]

I was standing just past the edge of a deteriorating asphalt road, the black tar long bleached out by the sun's radiation and the wind's constant dusting with the powdery, biscuit-colored sand that finds its way everywhere, into everything, crack or crevice. I was reading these words out

---

1. Mildred de Stanley, *The Salton Sea: Yesterday and Today* (Los Angeles, CA: Triumph Press, 1966), p. 3.

loud from the introduction of *The Salton Sea: Yesterday and Today* by Mildred de Stanley. It was a dramatic gesture that seemed false, my reading out loud to the barren landscape, but I'm prone to acting the way I think it would be cool to act in a situation with dramatic potential, instead of actually *experiencing* it.

It was one hundred and eleven degrees and so bright I squinted to read the page—and squinted when I looked back up at the desert around me, trying to match the description in the book with the landscape. Mildred de Stanley's location, geographically, was right near where I stood, but historically it was fifty years ago. She was seeing marinas and luxury homes, and I was seeing a desert with occasional fist-size chunks of ancient concrete and a few sickly date palms. Beyond the palms, the biscuit-colored sand ran up to a pale blue gash across the horizon, then to the Chocolate Mountains under the big, relentless sky.

Mildred de Stanley's book reads like the script to a film-strip found in an abandoned back room of the chamber of commerce. It seems more like propaganda than information. Published in 1966, it tells the whole story of Imperial Valley, from ancient geological shifting and shaking, through the creation of the Salton Sea, "born of a man's mistake," to the "courageous men who struggled to make a home on the inhospitable desert and developed a land of marinas and luxury homes that seems like no other."[2] The entire story is told in definitive, dramatic statements mixed with near-verbatim reports from the California State Fish and Game Department and the Imperial Irrigation District.

---

2. de Stanley, *The Salton Sea: Yesterday and Today*, p. 3.

Near the end, the narrative collapses into sections of travel guide, ads for local businesses, hunting and fishing regulations, photographs, and full-on boosterism randomly interspersed. Fifty years later, the book had a weird vibe I couldn't quite figure out. I was reading a sales pitch, but I didn't mind, since a sales pitch was the reason I came here in the first place.

HOW DID WE get so far away from who we thought we were, from who we thought God was? From the beginning, we kept moving, spreading out, dominating the land. We felt driven: civilize, build, educate, and innovate. Not satisfied, we wanted to do more, learn more, add a deck onto the house, take part of Ukraine. Before we knew it, we were a long way from where we started. But this is what we do—and maybe part of that came from God's whisper in our ear. After all, it's the first thing he ever told us to do: *Be fruitful and multiply, and fill the earth and subdue it; and have dominion over the fish of the sea and over the birds of the air and over every living thing that moves upon the earth.*[3]

But God didn't tell us how or why. God planted an impulse in us we don't understand. It drives us to move out, to conquer the barren wilderness, to establish new nations, to angle for more likes and retweets—to move further away, higher up, subdue and have dominion.

In fact, just six chapters into the book of Genesis, this spreading out and dominating of the earth spun out of control. People were increasing and spreading out too fast. They

---

3. Genesis 1:28, in *The Holy Bible; Revised Standard Version Containing the Old and New Testaments, with the Apocrypha/Deuterocanonical Books* (New York: Collins, 1973).

were multiplying—hooking up and having baby humans—filling up the land, and moving on.

Not only was there increasing and multiplying, but the humans and the angels were also hooking up and producing giant babies—I mean baby giants: angels and humans mating produced the Nephilim, a race of giants. The text says, "The Nephilim were on the earth in those days . . . when the sons of God [those are the angels] went in to the daughters of humans, who bore children to them. These were the heroes of old, the men of renown."[4]

The heroes of old, the men of renown. Heroes of old? Time was just getting started. People hadn't been around long enough to *make* ancient history. Not long enough for renown, acclaim, distinction, eminence, glory, honor. The Heroes of Old, the Men of Renown—it sounds like a movie starring Sean Connery and Morgan Freeman.

Whatever the Nephilim did to earn their renown, God didn't like it. In fact, God didn't seem to like anything that humans were doing. "The LORD saw that humanity had become thoroughly evil on the earth and that every idea their minds thought up was always completely evil. The LORD regretted making human beings on the earth, and he was heartbroken. So the LORD said, 'I will wipe off of the land the human race that I've created: from human beings to livestock to the crawling things to the birds in the skies, because I regret I ever made them.'"[5]

Reading this makes me feel bad for God. He was going

---

4. Genesis 6:4, in *The Holy Bible; Revised Standard Version Containing the Old and New Testaments, with the Apocrypha/Deuterocanonical Books*.

5. Genesis 6:5-7, in *Common English Bible: A Fresh Translation to Touch the Heart and Mind* (Nashville: Common English Bible, 2011).

to blot out everything he had made—all the people, all the animals, all the birds, all the crawling things—because he was sorry he had made them. All that creating, and now everything was ruined.

As bad as it was for God, it was worse for everything he had created. What did the animals and the creeping things and the birds ever do? And wasn't it the angels God should be mad at? After all, it takes two to make a man-of-renown baby giant. Humans weren't making giants on their own.

God was upset by people increasing and spreading all over the earth—*but he told them to do it.* On the sixth day of creation. It was the first thing God ever said to humans after creating and blessing them.

They did what they were created to do. There weren't a lot of rules at that point, basically just the two: Do not eat that fruit and be fruitful. When people started being super-fruitful and multiplying and spreading out over the earth and having all kinds of dominion, they didn't know it was going to lead to their wickedness being great all over the earth—and no one could have seen the sex-with-angels-thing coming.

Sure, mistakes were made in the Garden, and people paid for them. But after that, before things really got out of hand, maybe God could have stepped in to give clearer guidance?

All the talking God was doing (about how he regretted making people and how he was going to destroy everything) was just internal monologue. But he sure found his voice when it came to plans for drowning everyone—well, except for the righteous Noah and his family. When God found Noah, God couldn't stop talking. The story goes on for four of the first nine chapters of the Bible. The story of the Great Flood, the Great Deluge. To get this much real estate, the story must be important. And this isn't the only flood story around; a lot of cultures have them. There are Mesopotamian flood stories, Greek and Native American versions. The flood is always the result of the evil people do. Zeus was just as fed up with people as God—he saved one old couple and sent a great flood to drown every other living thing.

What makes a story so important that it shows up so many places and has so much weight in the opening chapters of our holy book? And why is it important for people to tell a story about a creator drowning them all for their wickedness? What did the people misunderstand when God told them to multiply and spread out over the earth? Clearly they did something wrong. But how did that grow out of fulfilling God's command?

God created us in God's image and nurtured us in the most intimate relationship with God, ourselves, other people, and the natural world. Then God separated us from all that glorious, naked propinquity and sent us off on our own for the first time with that command—so we did our best to fulfill it, and it made God want to kill us all (well, not quite all of us). It seems to me that newly created, self-reflecting life forms who are part dust and part God-breath could be forgiven for not understanding what they were supposed to do right off the bat.

I FOUND Mildred de Stanley's book after Connie Barrington, the head librarian for Imperial County, sent me to the Salton City Branch of the Imperial County Library. In addition to finding Grandpa Webb's plot, I wanted to find the stories, the substrate of this place. I wanted to know everything about the resort developments, all the way back to the flood.

After hearing and retelling the Salton Sea flood stories for so long, I was curious to see how close these were to the historical records. The library had some historical accounts that were out of print and unavailable elsewhere. Librarian Barrington also recommended books and locals to talk to. As I learned long ago, a librarian, part accountant and part hunter, is an excellent starting point for a search.

Before the Interweb, I used to call up the reference experts at the St. Paul Public Library and ask them all kinds of questions, and they would always find the answers. It was like Google, but with real people and no robot algorithms trying to monetize search results. So I trusted Librarian Barrington.

It's an unusual thing to have to actually travel to a particular place to find information about that place. But I like it. It's not convenient, but you don't need to know what you're looking for to find it. No amount of typing into search engines could conjure up the books and information I wanted.

I had to actually be there.

I wasn't looking for Mildred de Stanley's book when I walked into the Salton City Branch Library. I had left the list of books I was searching for at the Brawley Inn, where Mike and I had set up base camp. When I imagined this trip, I envisioned myself as my exemplar, Sarah Vowell, the social observer, cultural critic, and author of quirky American history books like *The Wordy Shipmates*, in which she uses irony, charming snarky-ness, and exhaustive research into niche areas of American history to explore questions about what it means to be imbedded in American culture in the present. (Vowell is also the voice of Violet in *The Incredibles*.)

I pictured myself being just like Sarah Vowell when she visits a historic site and meets a local character. She charms said character with unbridled enthusiasm and informed sarcasm, at which point he or she reveals a previously unknown, oddly poignant detail.

But when I opened the door of the library and stepped inside, I felt like I had walked into a stranger's living room. I couldn't muster unbridled enthusiasm or informed sarcasm. The three people in the library stopped what they were doing and looked at me. The library clerk behind the desk just inside the door, who might have been twenty, said hi. "Um," I replied, failing to channel Ms. Vowell, looking for my list of books, opening and closing my Moleskine several times, as if performing a magic trick for myself unsuccessfully: *As you can see, the list is not here. Watch as I close my planner and reopen it to find . . . it is still not here.*

"Um," I said again. I talk a lot. I guess you could say I talk for a living, but I'm acutely anxious in situations where I don't know people or don't know the governing social norms or rules. But the clerk smiled. I told him that I was doing research, that I was interested in the Salton Sea–Riviera period of local history. "You know, when there were, supposedly, country clubs and yacht clubs and amazing vacation lots for sale."

He pointed to the back and said he thought there were some books there, but then turned around to the shelf behind him, saying, "There was this one book. . . ." He found it and handed it to me. Faded from sitting in the rack near the front window for years on end, it looked like a travel brochure. When I flipped through it, I knew immediately that this was what I was looking for. Washed-out historic

27

photos, hand-drawn illustrations, maps, pages of contemporary (sixties) black-and-white photographs of marinas and clubs and people playing on the California Riviera. And lots of exclamation marks. The book was both a history of and an artifact from the time.

When I asked the clerk if he knew where I could buy a copy, he said no and held out his hand. Reluctantly I gave him the book. He looked at the cover, flipped the book over and looked at the back, then put it on the desk in front of him and slid it across to me. "You could probably just have it. I know we have another copy somewhere."

I picked it up, pressed it between my hands in the praying gesture, and thanked him. "Are you from a cable show or something?" he asked. My first instinct was to say yes. I thought maybe he wanted me to be from a cable show, so I wanted that for him for a second, but he had been genuinely nice and helpful, so I told him the truth: no. If he would have asked if I was from "This American Life," it might have been harder to resist the instinct to pretend.

I told him I was doing research on the Salton Sea, and I wanted to see the ruins of the glory days. "Oh, cool," he said. It was noon, and he had to close the library for lunch. "Come back later if you want." I thanked him again and pogoed to the car, silently thanking Sarah Vowell.

THE THINGS PEOPLE are willing to pretend to see, to believe, or to understand are astounding. We ache to belong, to be a part of something important, meaningful, valuable. And I don't think it comes from some naïve after-school-special, peer-pressure motivation. Its first building block is a deep desire to re-member our selves to some subconscious relationship, maybe even that state in Paradise before God, woman, man, and soil were separated.

The etymology of the word "relationship" includes the ideas of again, of bringing a previous state back into being, restoring; and also telling, connecting by telling, making a claim on a person, place, or state by reporting or proclaiming. So there's a lot below the surface of my cry of "Look at me—don't you think I'm just like Sarah Vowell?" And Grandpa Webb and Mildred de Stanley doing whatever they could to be a part of the hottest real estate development in the history of the Southern California desert.

Standing in that desert, I marveled at the audacity of the ambition Mildred de Stanley recites. "It is hard to believe that this land of sparkling turquoise blue, of marinas and luxury homes, was an uninhabited desert wasteland only a little more than seventy years ago. Those times are so strange and so far removed from our way of life, that they seem unbelievable."[6]

The audacity of ambition. Is it the secret whispering of God that compels it, or is it a fundamental misunderstanding of what it means to fill the earth and dominate it?

I shielded my eyes with the open book and watched Mike, who had walked off but was now hurrying back to where I stood. He had a sour, moving-toward-revolted look on his face—and then it hit me too. The wind had shifted, and the smell coming off the Salton Sea was cadaverous. The stench was aggressive, volitional. It chased us back to my Prius, parked in the middle of the empty, crumbling road.

---

6. de Stanley, *The Salton Sea: Yesterday and Today*, p. 3.

CHAPTER 3

Too Close, Too Soon . . .

Deng Xiaoping's China . . .

The Great Tower of Babel . . .

The Making of Madame Mao . . .

An Endless City of Shining Towers and

Crumbling Buildings . . .

Of all the legendary man-made objects you can see from outer space, the Great Wall of China is the original, the benchmark, the inceptive claim. From the distance of history and geography, time and space, I had seen the Wall. I had seen photographs and documentary films. I had read about it in textbooks, novels, short stories, and news magazines. In fact, I had been obsessed with the Wall and all things China since I was a teenager. But from a distance, I was only seeing ideas about the Great Wall—which are important, but abstract. Seeing things from a distance is about thinking, which I love to do, but seeing things close up is a fully sensual way of considering a something, a someplace. It is smelling and hearing and touching, looking close and running a finger along a crack to understand where it starts. I was impressed that the Salton Sea and the Great Wall of China are visible from outer space. But I longed to know them close up.

And finally, after years of dreaming about going to China, I actually got the chance to do it. Through a nursing student exchange at my wife Jeanne's school, we had found a semi-affordable way to make the trip with our two kids, Maria and Joe. They had been going to a Chinese language immersion school for six years, and we wanted them to be able to try speaking Chinese in a Chinese-speaking country. We had a plan. Jeanne would go to school during the day while the kids and I explored. When she completed her class, we would travel for three weeks after that. I was excited to see the Great Wall and immerse myself in the culture that Qin Shi Huangdi created when he unified the seven kingdoms, and to see how that unity was translated, by way of Mao, into contemporary Communist China.

That first night, after a long drive from the airport, we arrived at Huzhou University housing. Unfolding ourselves from the van, we dragged our luggage onto the sidewalk in front of the modern-ish, state architecture-styled structure (think Soviet Bloc). The one glass door that wasn't missing said "Doors locked between 10pm and 6am."

Our apartment was on the top floor of a nine-story building near the center of campus—the English sign in front calls it "The Expert Building," designating it for visiting scholars, foreign teachers, and students. But the people here didn't look very foreign—or very scholarly.

As we made our way to the elevator, a naked man (the building manager, we later learned) stepped out of a room by the stairs, looked at us, scratched himself, and went back inside. He lived in the room behind the front desk, apparently with two women. There was a sheet stretched across the middle of the room to separate the bed from the, um, other part. I was no longer seeing China from a distance; this was close up.

Too close, too soon.

We finally got our bags unpacked in our small apartment and started settling in. But four hours after my wife and I had put the kids to bed, Maria woke up crying. She was scratching and wailing that something kept biting her. That woke all of us—and we all started itching. None of us went back to sleep. As the sun was coming up, Jeanne went next door to get the director of the nursing exchange program. He brought a flashlight, stripped the beds, and examined the mattresses. Bedbugs.

I went out on the balcony on the ninth floor of the Expert Building and watched Huzhou come out of the darkness. In the near distance I saw a small mountain and could make out the Buddhist monastery I had read about. Then, as the early sun brought the rest of the city to light, I saw tower cranes— seven, twelve, twenty tower cranes, one footed—plunged into an endless city of shining towers and crumbling buildings. People emerged, seemingly from the soil. Then came the food carts, scooters, and bicycles as a market materialized on the high street below. Loud, blunt-edged voices and rancid smells reached me as the morning light came full, and now I could see a vast city covered in a patina of coal dust and cooking oil. I felt faint and put my hand on the balcony rail. It was sticky.

I realized this was no longer Mao's Communist China— it was Deng Xiaoping's China. And I might have really over-romanticized what this trip was going to be.

AT THIS POINT in the history of Genesis, the Tower of Babel is the biggest thing people have ever made. It's the first major human building project that's recorded. And it's ambitious. The ark doesn't really count—that was God's idea and design, and God only let Noah and his family work on it. The rest of humanity just laughed at Noah and went about their business, unaware of the impact their inability to swim would have on their near future.

The entire story of the Tower of Babel is only nine verses long in the eleventh chapter of Genesis, but it is a nearly universally recognized story. Besides the telling in Genesis, there are similar stories in the Koran and in Sumerian, Babylonian, Incan, Hungarian, and Irish folklore. It is the subject of operas, ballets, plays, and countless paintings throughout history—most famously, the Flemish master Brueghel's 1563 rendition of the Tower of Babel, patterned after the Roman Coliseum.

What is it about the story that continues to resonate over time? Is it because it's a compelling story of origin or *pourquoi* tale, like how the leopard got his spots or why a snake doesn't have legs? This story does explain why people are spread out all over the world and speak different languages. That must be part of it—but there's more. There's something about humanity's striving and perceived hubris in building a tower that reaches all the way to touch the heavens, to touch God. And there's also a powerful underlying tension generated by God's discomfort with the unity of people.

According to the rabbis, a span of two generations and 339 years separates the Flood and its aftermath from the building of the Tower, but Babel is the next bit of the story that Genesis narrates.

The people are unified, speaking one language, working

together with one purpose, which generally is considered a good thing. But God is angry, the way he was when people were being fruitful and multiplying and spreading all over the earth. God doesn't like this tower project.

Fresh from the flood, the whole earth is devastated, and the people come together and get busy making the best of a bad situation. The Genesis texts says that everyone on earth was one and spoke the same language, and that they all decided to head east together until they found this place in the flatlands, the desert of Shinar. They all agreed that it was a good place to put down roots, so they said, "Let's all make bricks and use some of this tar for mortar. And let's build ourselves a city—together."

You can practically hear the cry go up: "Yeah! All right! We're building ourselves a city. Let's do this thing!" Just your average, run-of-the-mill, rah-rah, let's-get-pumped-up affair. But then someone adds, "And let's build a tower that reaches all the way up to heaven. Let's make a name for ourselves. Otherwise we'll be scattered all over the face of the earth!" All the pumped-up people with their fists in the air start yelling, "Yeah!" then trail off and look at each other, puzzled. . . . "A tower that reaches heaven? Why would we. . . ? Is that even possible? Wait. What does that even mean—'make a name for ourselves'? Who are we trying to impress? We're the only people on earth."

Then a man in the crowd, a little panicked, asks, "What do you mean—'otherwise we'll be scattered all over the face of the earth'?" A woman, seeing where this thread is going, picks it up: "So you're saying that if we don't make a name for ourselves with this crazy tower thing, we'll be scattered all over the face of the earth? Far away from this place, far away from each other? How could that happen? Who could . . ." Then it dawns on her, and she whispers, "You mean"—she points up, but covers the gesture with her other hand—"him?"

After the Great Flood, God and humanity seem to have a lot of unresolved feelings about each other. God is at a loss. What else can he do? He threw them out of the garden, but that didn't teach them. He thought for sure everyone would straighten up after he basically destroyed the whole earth with a flood. But as soon as there was a little bit of dry land, they started right back at it—the same behavior. Now he can't really do the flood thing again because he promised he wouldn't. But that was as much because it didn't have the desired effect as it was compassion. As for the people—well, it's hard for them to forget that God nearly wiped all of them out. Sure, he promised he wouldn't do it again, but it's always in the back of their minds.

Now God mostly keeps to himself, keeps his distance, and the people focus on figuring some things out on their own. Sure, they're polite when they see each other, but they keep the conversation light, tiptoe around any subjects having to do with disobedience or the weather forecast. Just one little mention that it looks like rain, and everybody gets upset all over again.

Building this tower and making a name for themselves could be a defensive move, some pre-emptive action to guard against God's next play—which they seem to think might be scattering them all over the face of the earth. So, just to be on the safe side, they create a place that reaches above the high-water mark. Or maybe they build the tower to reach outer space, because that's where God is. They're out in the desert, looking up, wondering if God is looking down, noticing them. Maybe what they mean by making a name for themselves is doing something that God would notice. They're building a tower that reaches outer space so they can, once again, see God close up.

The story continues with the Lord actually coming down (from heaven? from outer space?) to see the city and the tower the people had built all by themselves, and he's impressed. Impressed, but a little . . . alarmed? Concerned? Then the Lord says (to himself? to the angels in heaven? to the reader?), "Look what they've done. They're all united, they're all one people, they all have one language. And they've built this tower. This is just their first project. Now nothing will stop them, nothing will be impossible—they'll be able to build whatever they want, do whatever they want. This isn't good."

In *Genesis Rabbah*, Rabbi Simeon b. Yohai says that this is one of only ten times the Lord comes down to earth from above. The first time, he came down to look for Adam and Eve in the Garden after the forbidden-fruit incident. When God comes down this time, he doesn't even go looking for the people. Instead, he seems to want to see what they've built—and he doesn't like what he sees.

Without a word to the people, he scatters them all over the face of the earth—and that's exactly what they were afraid the Lord would do. He also—and this they didn't see coming—confuses their language. Now they can't understand each other, and so they can't work together. They are no longer one people, united, with one language. They are divided and diverse. God has put distance between them.

MY FAMILY AND I got more bad news about the Huzhou University housing: it had no Wi-Fi, no Internet access—it barely had plumbing. And even though Huzhou is a city of more than a million people and the university has a campus of 17,000 students and faculty, no wireless fidelity existed. My laptop and phone were useless for getting online. We were also informed by our Communist Party escort that not only were we not allowed to use the library computers, but that the library didn't have any computers for us not to use. And it turned out that foreigners weren't allowed in Internet cafés without a Chinese ID, which was impossible to get.

So here I was, finally in the country I had dreamed about, besieged by frustration and loneliness. I felt so far away from everyone and everyplace I knew.

Soon I transgressed the "no foreigners in the Internet café" law; I was desperate. I felt overwhelmed by China. It was loud and frantic, and I could feel it on my skin. I wanted to get close to something familiar, away from where I actually was.

The place I ventured into looked more like a dive bar than the urban hipster haunt I've come to associate with the term "café." It was crowded with teenage boys who were chain-smoking, pounding energy drinks, and yelling into their headsets at the other gamers. I gave the scowling man behind the counter 100 RMB and said, "Zhongquo bu hao," thinking that if I overpaid a little and ingratiated myself with my limited Chinese, I could persuade him to help me out. As it turns out, "Zhongquo bu hao" doesn't mean "I'm sorry—my Chinese is very bad"; it means "Chinese people are very bad." Which might have had something to do with the scowling. But he took the money, which I figured out later was more than a little overpaying.

Scowling Man set me up at a computer, cast a last look

of disdain my way, and returned to his station behind the counter. Immediately, about fifteen of the chain-smoking boys crowded around me, reading over my shoulder, leaning on each other and the back of my chair, making comments and laughing. I made a few attempts to communicate the inappropriateness of looking at someone's private emails. I kept repeating, "Bu hao, bu hao, bu hao, bu hao." And I made a gesture of covering up the screen with my hands and then a pushing-to-the-side movement, followed by pointing to them and then covering my eyes. I did all of this in a very fluid, stylized manner, of course, attempting to reference Peking Opera, to use a more indigenous form of hand gesturing.

What they saw, I'm sure, wasn't an attempt to communicate some basic etiquette concerning privacy and personal space. Instead, they saw a foreigner enter the bar, curse the Chinese people, hand over a ridiculous amount of money, and then sit down and have a slow-motion seizure while chanting, "Bad, bad, bad . . . bad, bad, bad." They laughed very loudly and called more chain-smokers over. To my credit, I only repeated the performance two more times. Then I wrote a few emails, including one to my editor, telling her that I was mistaken, that I wouldn't be in regular contact while I was in China.

Now I was even more dispirited. Where was the China I had read about, carried in my imagination all these years? The stories and the history that had always fascinated me came back to me in a Huzhou haze.

JIANG QING (pronounced Chiang Ching) was just twenty-four when she met Mao Zedong, but she had already been married three times and had worked for the Chinese Communist Party for seven years. She was also one of China's biggest movie stars. Jiang was a major celebrity in the thirties, starring in films and theater, even playing Nora in Ibsen's *A Doll's House* in Shanghai. At age fourteen, she joined an experimental theater school in Jian, the city where her mother had brought her after her father, abusive and alcoholic, died. Her mother made her living on the street, often dragging Jiang along with her. The theater school was a chance to get far away from the life she had been born into. A chance to imagine another life.

There is a trick of the imagination, a projection where you can see yourself as you hope you might be—a person who could matter, or was different, or could be noticed. And then you come back to yourself and start living as if you were that person—or at least attempting to live that way, motivated by that imagined, projected self. It's a trick that Jiang Qing used to her full advantage.

She impressed her instructors, and they recommended her for a prestigious acting scholarship in Beijing. There Jiang Qing found a cosmopolitan city with burgeoning pockets of intellectuals and artists. And in the late 1920s in Beijing—like New York, Paris, and every other major city in the world—where there were theater students, there were fervent young Communists drunk on art and ideology. Jiang Qing met and fell in love with Yu Qiwei, a member of the underground Communist Party's propaganda department. Together they fought the good fight. There was music in the cafés at night and revolution in the air.

At that time, the Chinese Communist Party and the Kuomintang (the Chinese Nationalist Party) were fighting the Japanese occupation and each other. With other artists, writers, and actors, Jiang Qing formed the Communist Cultural Front and performed *Put Down Your Whip!* on the streets. The play tells the story of a father and his daughter who escape from Japanese-occupied northeastern China with nothing, so they must perform on the streets, begging for money and bread. Soon the daughter becomes weak from hunger and falls to the ground, unable to go on.

But her father commands her to continue. He takes out a whip, striking her and shouting at her to get up, with the gathered crowd watching. As the father raises the whip one more time, high over his head, an angry young worker steps out of the masses and shouts, "Put down your whip!"—at which point the father comes to himself and breaks down in tears. The daughter immediately comes to her father's defense, telling the young worker and those gathered how devastating and dehumanizing life was under the oppressive occupation of the Japanese, how her father had become so broken and desperate from starvation and abuse that he was reduced to beating the daughter he loved in the street.

Feeling great pity for both father and daughter, the young worker makes an impassioned speech, exhorting the people to resist the Japanese. Then the cast, including the young worker, the father, and the daughter, turn to the audience gathered in the street and implore them to take up the cry "Down with Japanese imperialism! Down with Japanese imperialism!"

Put Down Your Whip! became wildly popular, and Jiang Qing made a name for herself. She not only began to become the person she longed to be, but also embodied something the Chinese people seemed to long for—to be able to stand up instead of being beaten down. Like the people who built the tower, the Chinese peasants were rising up: they too wanted to make a name for themselves.

The play was performed in cities all over China. It was like a Chinese Communist *Our Town*—it didn't require a big budget for sets and costumes, and no matter what the skill level of the actors, it always delivered an emotional wallop. *Put Down Your Whip!* was Jiang Qing's ticket to becoming one of China's biggest stars in theater and film. And her fame allowed her to meet—and marry—Mao Zedong.

THE GLORIOUS united China that Qin Shi Huangdi saw in his dream was fractured by the Japanese occupation. Mao Zedong and Deng Xiaoping fought with the same appetite for revolution, but had different convictions about what a united, communist China should look like.

The visions of these two men collided in the Long March, a 6,000-mile, 370-day retreat of the Red Army of China's Communist Party, with the Nationalist Army on its heels. The march ended with Mao Zedong ardently established as the leader of the Communist Party of China. To Deng Xiaoping's dismay, the scared, starving peasant soldiers preferred a charismatic visionary of the proletariat revolution as their leader. Deng believed that collaboration and interaction with the West and the Soviet Union could bring China into the elite community of the world's industrial and economic powers. For Mao, the highest value was a united peasant class and revolutionary purity.

When the People's Republic of China was officially founded in 1949, Mao Zedong controlled virtually every office of power. Deng's fortunes rose and fell depending on how vocally he opposed Mao. But then Mao's "Great Leap Forward," an economic and social campaign that lasted from 1958 to 1961, was a great failure. That gave Deng the chance to shift policies toward a more market-based economy; in fact, Deng is credited with bringing China back from near total collapse.

But Mao fought back. Fearing that Deng's reforms would bring back right-wing capitalism and kill the revolution, Mao re-asserted his power and had Deng "criticized" and sent to work as a laborer in a truck factory. Mao then instituted the Cultural Revolution in 1966, essentially turning the country over to the Gang of Four, with Jiang Qing—now his wife, "Madame Mao"—leading the way.

But the revolution—a campaign to purify the country of all academics and business professionals and to end contact with the rest of the world—didn't improve the economy. By the end of the ten-year nightmare, Mao was dead, and Deng was able to out-maneuver Madame Mao and the Gang of Four. With his allies, Deng took complete control of China. At last, Deng was able to implement what he called his "socialism with Chinese characteristics."

WHEN DENG ROSE to power in 1978, he opened the country to foreign investment and established what he called Special Economic Zones. The SEZ were a state-planned field of dreams for rabid, prancing capitalists. And did they come. The first SEZ was established in Shenzhen, a sparsely populated area known historically for its salt fields. The powdery, biscuit-colored soil was so important to the salt trade that it was put under imperial protection during the Han dynasty. Shenzhen literally means "deep drain," because of the geological depression that defined the area. During the rainy season, the water from the surrounding hills would run through it in streams.

In 1984, the Chinese Communist Party laid out the plans to transform the small border village of Shenzhen into a new mega-city. Next, billions of dollars and a million workers began to create a modern industrial and commercial center on the Shenzhen plain. Deng ordered the construction of a 68-mile chain-link fence, topped with razor wire, along the northern border of Shenzhen. It was designed to keep Chinese peasants from entering the Special Economic Zone and looking for work without permission.

When the SEZ was first established, the tallest structure in the region was five stories. Within a decade, there were 300 skyscrapers, including the tallest building in China at the time: the 53-story International Trade Center, built in just 18 days, complete with a revolving penthouse restaurant.

In the center of the city a soaring tower was built, reaching almost to the heavens; it included a Walmart Supercenter. In the 1990s Shenzhen's motto was "One high-rise a day, one boulevard every three days." And today the tower-building continues, seemingly endless. Shenzhen is home to China's 9th and 14th tallest towers, the world's 12th and 21st tallest. Scores of other towers are either completed or under construction.

In just over twenty years, Shenzhen has grown to a population of 14 million. It is China's third-largest and richest per-capita city, its busiest container port, and the fastest-growing city in the world. It is also China's most dangerous city—even more dangerous than Shanghai, the largest city in the world. In addition, according to Jonathan Alter of *Newsweek*, "It is also a pit, lacking not just Hong Kong's charm but its coherence. The capitalism there is too unbridled and unanchored in laws; the buildings erected only five years ago are already falling down."[1]

This isn't surprising. Many of the buildings were constructed with steel, which is now corroding because of the high salt content in the local sand. That, combined with the shoddy work of masses of inexperienced laborers and the extreme time pressures, produced buildings and roads that began to crumble shortly after they were completed. And the signs of ruin are everywhere. The pollution levels often make the air painful to breathe, and the Pearl River, which runs through Shenzhen, is so brown and thick it is easy to imagine you could walk across its surface.[2]

I'm sure that Shenzhen is very impressive from above, all those towers, like one massive, immovable power, glinting in the sun. But on the ground it's easier to see the stained streets, the crumbling foundations, and the everyday exhausted people who, no matter how far back they crane their necks, will never be able to see the top of any tower.

---

1. Alter, quoted in Jeffrey Hays, "Shenzhen and the Pearl River Delta." http://factsanddetails.com/china/cat15/sub96/item469.html. Accessed July 2015.

2. Jeffrey Hays, "Shenzhen and the Pearl River Delta." http://factsanddetails.com/china/cat15/sub96/item469.html. Accessed July 2015.

CHAPTER 4

Ever Get the Feeling You've Been Cheated? . . .
An Illusion Masking Our Desire for Real Connection . . .
The Orbiting Self . . .
The Pioneers' Park Museum . . .
The Colorado River Stopped Draining
into the Desert . . .

I know the Industrial Revolution really messed things up. Folks used to work together with their families and neighbors. They would plant in the spring and harvest in the fall. They would make whatever they needed—chairs or butter or knives or clothes. Then machines got invented, and our folks moved to cities to work in factories and run the machines. They didn't work with their families and neighbors anymore, season by season, and they didn't make things for themselves anymore. So they no longer saw the rhythm and the meaning in their work. They pounded a rivet all day and then went home. But at least they got to go home.

Standing at the dawn of the Digital Revolution, I am exhausted. It was all supposed to be such a good thing. I could have a personal, powerful digital device connecting me constantly to my family, my friends—and the whole freakin' world. But as the power drains from my laptop, I can feel the power draining from me.

Remember when we used them to interact with other people, to connect, to communicate, before the devices we put between us started taking something from us? I can't put my finger on exactly what it is the devices take as they pass our conversations back and forth for us. It feels like energy, humanity, emotion, or meaning—whatever it is that makes us fully alive. The devices mediate our relationships.

The dominance of digitally mediated interactions is little more than a decade old. Facebook was founded in 2003, Twitter in 2006. We're only beginning to understand the spiritual and cultural effects. At first it was all convenient, occasional, and fun. But now "occasional" no longer seems like an option. And the fun is gone. The constant demands of living in an ever-expanding Digital Empire leave me feeling overwhelmed, powerless, and alienated.

How can the almost constant connection to some sort of virtual community filled with "friends" and "followers" and the ability to seek out people with your exact interests and ideas meet the need for real connection? Our digital lives provide us with an illusion that masks our desire for real connection—to others, the created world, and the creator (and one-time flooder) of that world.

LET'S GO BACK two thousand years. Before the Digital Empire, before the Industrial Revolution, to the Roman Empire. To a time when Jesus was wrangling with naysayers and making new connections.

Near the end of the Gospel of Matthew, the Pharisees are questioning Jesus, trying to trip him up, hoping he'll say something blasphemous or treasonous so they can have him arrested. "One of them, a legal expert, tests him. 'Teacher, what is the greatest commandment in the Law?'"[1]

That question isn't as easy as you might think. Sure, Christians have just the Ten Commandments—but Jews find 613 in the Hebrew Bible. Still, Jesus doesn't bat an eye. The greatest commandment? Number one? "You shall love the Lord your God with all your heart and with all your soul and with all your mind." Then he gives them another one. "You shall love your neighbor as yourself." All 613 laws, everything the Lord our God commanded through the prophets—all depend on these two. Love God with all that you are, and love your neighbor. That's it.

Now Jesus turns the tables by asking the Pharisees a question: "What do you think about the Messiah? Whose son do the prophets say he is?" That's easy to answer, they say, rolling their eyes. The Messiah is the son of David.

Jesus follows up: If the Messiah is the son of David, then how is it that in the Psalms David says about the Messiah, "The Lord said to my Lord, sit at my right hand until I make your enemies your footstool"? David is calling the Messiah his Lord, but no one would ever call their son their Lord. Jesus probably resists rolling his eyes, but his tone of voice says it all.

The Pharisees are stumped. They think, *Wait a minute—how can that work? The Messiah can't be both David's Lord and David's son. That would be impossible—a contradiction. But our holy book says both things.* The Pharisees are now not only embarrassed, but unsure—and undone.

---

1. Matthew 22:35-36, in *Common English Bible: A Fresh Translation to Touch the Heart and Mind* (Nashville: Common English Bible, 2011).

Their whole platform, their whole system is built on their surety. Knowing what's right and what's wrong, knowing the correct interpretation of the law and the prophets—these are the foundation of their beliefs. And not only their beliefs but the religious system (the towers, you might say) they have put in place. This is why they love lists. They love order. In a world where the Roman Empire has invaded and occupied their country, they desperately want to make order out of the chaos of that situation. Strict rules. Lists of how people should behave. And they're in luck, because the Romans value order. Empires abhor chaos.

Without order, without lists, rules, laws—empires can't exist. So Jesus—an empire breaker—questions the very assumption that ranking, listing, and ordering things equals what is good, what is right. And he rejects the assumption that the commands of God, God's words to God's people—God's interaction with God's people—can be contained, can be controlled, can be placed in a proper ranking order. That's why Jesus asked a question that has two right and opposing answers—it's the opposite of a list. It's the opposite of ranking. What is the greatest commandment? Jesus says it doesn't work that way. Jesus' answer doesn't bring order out of chaos—it pushes out further into the chaos. It is destabilizing.

Though the Pharisees are no doubt deaf to it, Jesus is saying something new about relationships, about connections both human and divine. Relationships are not quantifiable. Love doesn't work that way. Real connections are fluid, changing, moving—and alive. They're not orderly and controllable; they require vulnerability and risk. They also require trust and thrive on mercy. They are the antithesis of lists.

CHINA USED TO be very far away—well, a long time ago, when I was in tenth grade. It wasn't only distant but so different and strange and suspect. Which is how I felt in high school (well, maybe now sometimes too), so I liked it.

I was on the freaks and geeks spectrum, but I never found a gang of misfits and outsiders to strike up unlikely friendships with, kids who would make it possible for me to negotiate high school successfully. But I did find a Gang of Four, the British post-punk band, which led me to the Gang of Four, the Chinese Communist political quartet that took the fall for the Chinese Cultural Revolution.

As much as the music, I liked the idea from which Gang of Four built their name: from these three Chinese Communists led by Mao's wife, who took control of the country and nearly destroyed it by implementing all these extremely insane policies. It seemed to resonate with the new regime I was living under in high school. It awed me—both that a band could be smart and edgy enough to name themselves after crazy Chinese Communists, and that just four people—the leader's wacky wife and her three wacky friends—could take over the most populous country in the world.

All of this bizarre history can now easily be found in an afternoon on the Internet. But when I was in high school, it took trips to the Oriental Studies section of the university library and the perusing of many peripheral books until I found something in one to point me to the other books I would need to read. At the time, current information about China was hard to come by, but more difficult than learning anything about it was just the absence of China in the cultural consciousness. It wasn't a superpower, it wasn't an economic power—in 1980 it ranked ninth in the world's largest economies, behind Italy, behind Canada. What people generally knew about China was this, more or less: they were Commies, Mao's Little Red Book was their Bible, Nixon went there, and the government would only let a married couple have one kid.

But in 1981, my first year of high school, not only did Gang of Four's second album, *Solid Gold*, come out, but the Gang of Four was on trial in China for anti-revolutionary activities during the Cultural Revolution. There wasn't much mention of Madame Mao's gang in the news—and even less mention of the album—but they somehow found their way into my consciousness. In my first year of high school I felt so weird and other that identifying with this strange band and this big, weird, other country that everyone in America thought of as unacceptable, if they thought of it at all, was just externalizing what I felt about myself. The band and China—they were right out there for everyone to see. Every day I wanted to be okay with being big, weird me, like the band, like China: out of the ordinary, beyond the mundane, and real. This music and this oriental history *meant* something. Of course I had no idea *what* they meant. I was in high school and discovering something a great distance away from my ordinary life; launching myself in its direction passed for meaning, for connection.

In *Lost in the Cosmos: The Last Self-Help Book*, novelist Walker Percy writes a fake twenty-question self-help quiz. Question 14 is "THE ORBITING SELF: Reentry Problems of the Transcending Self, or Why it is that Artists and Writers, Some Technologists, and indeed Most People have so much Trouble Living in the Ordinary World." The possible answers go on and on, like the question, but Percy does seem to address my adolescent launching problem and suggests it probably persists into adulthood.

He says the Orbiting Self is someone disconnected from ordinary life who seeks to make a real connection to God, to the other people in their lives, or to the world they move through—any kind of real connection would do. They want to transcend the ordinary, to find the authentic. By engaging in a yoga retreat or a poetry class or attending the film society lectures, the Orbiting Self launches up out of the ordinary into the real.

The problem, Percy says, is that after the Orbiting Self achieves this moment of real connection, there is the next moment. The re-entry into the ordinary. "What goes up must come down. The best film of the year ends at nine o'clock. What to do at ten? What did Faulkner do after writing the last sentence of *Light in August*? Get drunk for a week. What did Dostoevsky do after finishing *The Idiot*? Spend three days and nights at the roulette table. What does the reader do after finishing either book? How long does his exaltation last?"[2]

FRANKLIN LEE WEBB was born in Oak Grove, Missouri, in 1916. His dad, Elmer, was as mean as you can imagine a mean dad during a depression, with the farm failing, the soil blowing away, with black storms roiling through everything.

"I think a lot got taken out on your grandpa," my mom told me once on the phone. I had called her to ask a few questions to fill in some gaps. "Your great grandma tried to

---

2. Walker Percy, *Lost in the Cosmos: The Last Self-Help Book* (New York: Picador, 2000), pp. 142-43.

protect him and got money from her side of the family to help him enroll in the airplane mechanic school."

Missouri Aviation Institute, in Kansas City, was one of many schools the government subsidized to provide training for placement in the airplane factories in California. The aviation schools gave young farm kids training in an industry that was growing and needed skilled workers.

After graduating, my grandpa headed for California. And he wasn't alone. Two and a half million people had fled the Dust Bowl states by 1940, with nearly a quarter of a million of them ending up in California looking for work. I don't know if I'm getting my grandpa's story mixed up with *The Grapes of Wrath*, but I'm pretty sure I remember that it was his diploma, which he carried folded up in his pocket, that got him past the armed road-blocks set up at the California border to keep more Okies from coming in. I guess it separated him from every other Tom, Dick, and Harry Joad. He had prospects.

When he got to San Diego, he was hired by Consolidated Aircraft. The job paid him enough to start a family, and by 1949 he moved them to a trailer out in the then-wild country of El Cajon.

THE WEBSITE FOR the Imperial County Historical Society Pioneers' Park Museum pointed out the museum's excellent historical research library and its availability to all researchers by appointment only. *I am a researcher*, I thought. *I will make an appointment.* A reviewer on TripAdvisor wrote, "Great history of the settlers and the region's water policies."[3] Not

---

3. DanielleK723, "Review of Imperial Valley Pioneers Museum," TripAdvisor, April 8, 2012: www.tripadvisor.com. Accessed April 8, 2012.

the kind of endorsement that usually excites prospective museum-goers, but it was exactly what I was looking for.

From my headquarters desk at the Brawley Inn, I emailed Leanne, the curator, explaining that I was researching the story of the accidental creation of the Salton Sea, and would be very interested in seeing the museum and the excellent historical library. And would she have any time to talk to me? She replied, thanking me for my interest, but explained that the archivist was away until December and the archives couldn't be made available on such short notice.

Wait—what? Sarah Vowell just shows up, and she never gets turned down. My niche-history researcher credentials were wobbling. Had my hubris done me in? Maybe Sarah Vowell doesn't just show up. It's possible that she makes appointments with curators of presidential assassination sites and Puritan archives, but doesn't include her scheduling emails in her books. *Rookie move on my part.* I looked out the window, past the sheer curtain dancing erratically in the full blast of an air conditioner fan on high, to the waves of heat coming off the black asphalt parking lot, and beyond, to the pool. Mike was the only one in it, and just his head, from his mouth up, was out of the water. He was wearing sunglasses and a hat. He did not look refreshed.

The curator and I exchanged another round of emails— same results. So, like the persistent researcher of niche history I was pretending to be, I called her and told that I just wanted to see the exhibits and the gift shop. "Well, of course," she said. "The museum is open until four."

I looked back at the website and saw the announced hours: *Open to the public from 10 am to 4 pm.* Maybe real, serious researchers of niche history go about things in a different way, a way I didn't know about. Why was finding out when I could go to a museum suddenly about my self-worth.

Mike had come into the room and changed. As he was tying his shoes, he asked, "Are we going to go to that museum today?" Yes, I told him. Right now.

The Pioneers' Park Museum is huge. A considerable two-story building houses the main exhibits on the agriculture and cattle business, the material on the aforementioned regional water system, a Colorado River/Salton Sea room, the ethnic galleries, and the gift shop.

It was quiet inside. And empty. A man and a woman chatted behind the main counter.

I saw a cash register sitting on the end of the counter closest to the door, so I walked over and stood in front of it. When I feel awkward in a situation and don't really know what to do, I often get in line to buy something. It always seems appropriate. I think this is why book tables at conferences and merch tables at concerts do most of their business. People are by themselves or feel out of place, they don't know what to do with themselves, so they look for something to buy. It's a clear and uncomplicated relationship. It's always okay to buy something. The woman came to the cash register, and I handed her my credit card to pay my entrance fee. She smiled and swiped it.

When she gave me my card back, I turned around and started walking purposefully toward something, for some reason trying to give the impression that I came here all the time and was heading off to see the thing I knew about, or do the thing I always did when I was here. That little bit of artifice brought me into the ethnic galleries. I began nodding my head, smiling, letting out a soft sound of recognition like "Yes" or "Ahh," but I think I actually mixed the two because I switched halfway through to a meaningful "Yaahh." I repeated it, nodding my head more emphatically, and now it sounded vaguely German. So when I saw a sign for the German gallery, I headed straight for it. Mike caught up with me while I was nodding at a display of artifacts from early German settlers and saying, "Yaahh—ya vol, ya vol."

"What are you doing?" Mike asked, puzzled.

"Um, just looking at the ethnic galleries. This is the German one." He told me he already knew that because of the German flag and the big sign on the wall that said "German." Then he began pointing at each large sign, each one above a nook of display cases, around the outside wall of the room. "And that is the Portuguese, Swiss, Korean, Japanese, Lebanese, Greek, Irish, Italian, French, Filipino, Mexican, African American, Indian, American Indian, and Chinese gallery."

Each is sponsored, I learned later, and independent. The sponsors determine and contribute the items displayed. Originally, nobody was actually from Imperial Valley—except a few of the Indian tribes. Everyone else came to America for the dream and to Imperial Valley because it had a pretty low buy-in to start making the dream come true. All you had to do was work really, really hard in nearly unlivable conditions. Even the native tribes going back many millennia only lived there half the year, moving up into the mountains in the summer.

I crossed over to the Chinese gallery. Ninety percent of the Chinese immigrants in Imperial Valley were from the south of China, including Guangdong Province. I remembered that the newly proclaimed Chairman Mao sent Deng

Xiaoping there to rout out Chiang Kai-shek and the Nationalists from their last stronghold. I wondered if that's when Deng hatched the idea that would become the SEZ of Shenzhen there, thirty years later?

When I wandered into the Colorado River/Salton Sea room, I discovered that the original canal, built to divert the Colorado River and irrigate the desert, was not the All-American Canal, as I remembered from my composite story, but the Alamo Canal, which was mostly in Mexico. After the flood, the All-American Canal was built as part of the Boulder Canyon Project Act of 1928, which was part of a major initiative to control future flooding in Imperial Valley. The project included building the Imperial Dam, which is where the Colorado is diverted into the All-American Canal, the Parker Dam, and the Hoover Dam. The All-American Canal, not to put too fine a point on it, was built all in America (the United States). It wasn't named as a tribute to the unity of all the Americas.

In the back of the ethnic galleries building, I found an entire corner gallery dedicated to Harold Bell Wright, the best-selling American author of the first quarter of the twentieth century. (This is what I learned from the display cards. I had never heard of him.) While he had many best-selling books, he was the first writer to become a millionaire through book sales alone and the first writer to sell a million copies of a book. The majority of the displays in this gallery are dedicated to his 1911 novel, *The Winning of Barbara Worth*.

I hadn't heard of Wright, but I knew Barbara Worth—or the name. There were all kinds of things named after her in Imperial Valley. As I explored the Wright gallery, reading the placards and sussing out the importance and relevance of the books, papers, and items on display, I was surprised to learn that Barbara Worth was the fictional protagonist of the novel. Figures. One of the area's most lauded citizens was fictional. The book was published just four years after the Colorado River stopped draining into the desert.

Only after I returned to my lair at the Brawley Inn and started Googling "Harold Bell Wright" and reading *The Winning of Barbara Worth* did I, to my pleasure and amazement, realize that everything in the novel was fictional, right down to the story of the flood and the creation of the Salton Sea.

CHAPTER 5

The Day God Learned Forgiveness . . .

A Sort of Lyrical World-Dominating Superpower . . .

This Massive Miscalculation . . .

Al J. Kalin, 1888-1951: Pioneer, Cattleman, Farmer,

Innovator, Builder, Visionary . . .

The rabbis have been riffing on the Noah story since they first heard it. All kinds of stories appear in the midrash of the ancient rabbis. And who doesn't like the stories about Noah and the animals? The animals, the pairs of every kind, two by two, make it a popular children's story. And that has to be the only reason it would be, because—well, you know, the whole bit about God wanting to kill every living thing isn't exactly warm and fuzzy.

The rabbis say that Noah, in preparing for his trip, not only gathered up the starter set of animals, birds, and creeping things, but also had to learn what all of them ate, so he could figure out what kinds of food to bring along. To do this, he had to watch them all, observe them, get to know them.

Once Noah loads up his family and brings in all the animals and what every living thing needs to eat, he shuts the ark, and the rain comes. It lifts the boat high away from land, so Noah has to spend the next 150 days shut up in that boat, feeding his family and feeding and taking care of the animals—all the living things. He's learned that certain animals have to eat at the third hour of the day, and certain animals have to eat at the sixth hour of the day, and in between all these feedings he's got to clean up. Because if you're going to give animals food, they're going to poop. As the ancient rabbis say, everybody poops. Giraffes, elephants, donkeys, doves, deer, antelope, anteaters, hippopotami, hyenas, pigeons—they all poop. And that's a lot of poop.

The rabbis say that after all that feeding and taking care of all the living things, after the continual cleaning up of their poop, Noah came to know all the animals really well, and it changed him. The act of nurturing the animals and birds and creeping things transformed him from the kind of human that was born to multiply, to spread out all over the earth and have dominion over everything, into a thoughtful, caring, intelligent kind of human. The kind of human that took the time to learn about all of creation, and as he cared for it, he came to care about it. Noah's time on the ark re-created him. After the 150-day gestation period in the womb that is the ark, Noah is born not as a dominator, not as a subduer of creation, but as a nurturer of creation.

There's another story from the rabbis which says that after the ark was sealed and the waters came and lifted it up, one of the Nephilim was treading water next to it. Yes, one of the half-human, half-angel giants who were part of what seemed to be the last straw of evilness for God—one of those Nephilim was treading water. Being a half-human and half-angel giant, he was able to tread water longer than regular people. This giant hero of old, this Man of Renown, swam to the ark, and with the tips of his fingers held on to the planking on the side of it, climbing just above water level. Through all the storms, through the rain and the wind, the giant held on. As his body was battered, he grunted and gasped—and Noah heard him. And when Noah ran up to the deck of the ark and looked over the side, he saw the Nephilim clinging there.

So Noah went back down into the ark and cut a small hole right next to the giant and made a little door, and every day Noah would open the little door and feed the Nephilim. Every day, after Noah fed all the living things inside the ark, he saved just a bit and then went to that little door, opened it, and fed the Nephilim. Noah did that until the day that the waters began to recede and the ark came to rest on dry land. Then the Nephilim dropped off the side and ran off into the distance.

Why did Noah feed the Nephilim? If God had wanted to save them, if God had intended they be a part of the re-creation, God would have instructed Noah to bring them into the ark. Was it that Noah, after feeding and caring for all the animals and birds and creeping things, couldn't help but feed any kind of creature that was hungry?

One thing for certain was God's reaction. God was angry. God got good and wrathful. God looked out and saw that Nephilim, that abomination born of the sin of men and of angels, and raised a lightning bolt to blast it off the side of the ark—but then God saw the little door open and watched Noah feed the Nephilim. At first God thought this was the ultimate betrayal by Noah, the one good man left, but as God watched him, day after day, open the little door and feed the Nephilim, God's heart softened. That is the power of acts of mercy—to reconnect, to mend what is broken. And

God decided right then and there not to kill the Nephilim. In fact, God decided never to destroy all the living things ever again—no matter what they did. Not the Nephilim, not Noah, not any other human, not the animals, or birds, or creeping things.

It was the first time that God, since the beginning of time, didn't respond to disobedience with just punishment. It was the day that God learned forgiveness.

QIN SHI HUANGDI, the teenage king, wanted to unify the warring kingdoms of China, creating one grand empire where he would rule and everyone would have to do everything exactly the same way. He would then build a wall around the empire, sit in the middle, and say, "Mine!"

Mao Zedong, the revolutionary people's leader, wanted to establish a sort of lyrical, world-dominating superpower where all were equal and did their part for the communal good, as he defined it. He wanted to use the masses like a calligraphy brush to express his political philosophies.

Social media and its interwebs have the power to be the great unifier. Everyone can have a voice and have access to unlimited information. Everyone can broadcast, write, publish, form groups, join, belong, and build their own social media empire.

But unity and equality don't necessarily go hand in hand. What starts as a beautiful, back-to-the-land commune can turn into a big drag of a rule-bound, fascist work farm before the first fava beans are harvested. In a community where one sets the parameters and dictates all the possibilities, real relationships, real connections, are nothing more than a dream.

AFTER THE FIRST Five-Year Plan of the newly established People's Republic was declared a success, Mao really wanted to pump up the volume on the modernization and industrialization project. During the first Five-Year Plan, patterned after that of the Soviet Union, the government had instituted land reforms, privatized industry, gotten the economy off to a pretty good start, and generally made things better for the majority peasant class. Next on Mao's list was to make his shiny new country a modern, industrialized state and a major player in the world export market.

China was closely following the Soviets' five-year plans, but Mao was apparently dissatisfied with their ongoing numerical designations (the first Five-Year Plan, the second Five-Year Plan, the third Five-Year Plan, etc.). As a poet, he reached for something a little more grand and inspirational. Even though the Soviet Union's no-nonsense designations served it well (well, that is, until its thirteenth Five-Year Plan was hosed due to the dissolution of the country), Mao instituted the Great Leap Forward instead of a second Five-Year Plan.

The country stood as though united at some starting line in history, poised, muscles coiled, ready to propel themselves by strength of will and body into the First World in one decisive movement. A great leap up and over the Great Wall onto the center stage of the industrialized world. The name of the new plan also implied leaping over things, as in skipping a few steps in the process, or leaping from a great height into the abyss. Unfortunately, the latter two images turned out to be more accurate.

The goal was to increase agricultural output by 270 percent and to become one of the world's major steel exporters. Given that China could barely produce enough food to feed its own people and wasn't really a steel exporter at all, that was quite a leap.

But the government was determined. It organized people into farming collectives and assigned them to grow a single crop, suitable for export. But China's farmers, accustomed to working their small farms with the livestock and crops necessary to do little more than feed their families, weren't used to large-scale industrial farming practices, and were so out of their element that agricultural production actually went down. And with the relatively few crops actually harvested being shipped off for sale, the collectives were increasingly unable to feed themselves.

ADDING TO THESE miscalculations, Mao instituted a public health campaign called the "Four Pests," aimed at eliminating rats, mosquitoes, flies, and sparrows. Mao was concerned about the country's hygiene, but he also wanted to use the campaign as a test of his extensive propaganda machine's ability to mobilize the entire country to serve a singular purpose. He marshaled his massive film, radio, and print crusades, as well as organizing troupes of children to perform plays and songs exhorting the people to band together in killing the "Four Pests."

One propaganda poster from the period shows a group of rosy-cheeked youngsters singing and dancing along. One little girl has a drum, another one has a pair of cymbals, while five little boys carry a flyswatter, one of those old-time pump-foggers for spraying poison indiscriminately into the air for all to breathe, a net, and a mop.[1] Cute. Another

---

1. Cheng Guoquan, 1961. "A Young Propaganda Troupe." Hebei Renmin

favorite speaks to the real unity the operation was meant to bring about. In the top of two panels are representative characters from any village or collective: several young and middle-aged men, a grandmother, a couple of young women, a few little boys, and a girl, all wearing variously colored Mao suits (with tunic-style jackets) and holding rifles. All of them are pointing their guns up into the same spot in a tree just out of the frame. Then in the bottom panel they're all gathered in a semi-circle, some down on one knee, one patting another on the back in congratulations. Holding their guns at jaunty angles, they look down with big, laughing smiles at a single small bird on its back on the ground. The caption reads, "Eliminating the last sparrow."[2]

The sparrow was labeled a grain-stealer, and there was just something special about killing sparrows that captured the national imagination. Schools, cooperatives, and public agencies would form groups and compete to see who could kill the most. By 1960 the Eurasian tree sparrow was virtually eliminated.

As charming and feel-good as that story seems, the goal of eliminating the last sparrow was never attained. People began to realize that while the sparrows might eat a little grain every now and then, their primary diet was insects. And without the sparrows to control them, great locust infestations destroyed millions of acres of crops. That, occurring in the midst of a long drought, pushed what was a drastic nationwide food shortage into a full-on famine.

Meishu Chubanshe. http://chineseposters.net/posters/pc-1961-004.php. Accessed January 14, 2015.

2. Shen Nan, 1959. "Eliminating the Last Sparrow." http://chineseposters.net/posters/e16-34.php. Accessed January 14, 2015.

The government removed the sparrow from the "Four Pests" campaign, replacing it with the bedbug. I can't imagine killing a bedbug brought people together in quite the same way.

The plan to dominate the global steel export market suffered from the same sort of massive miscalculation. In their second Five-Year Plan, the Soviet Union had successfully made the country into an industrial power almost overnight, creating huge steel foundries to forge girders for bridges and buildings and super-cool modern-industrialized-country things. Mao saw this as the next challenge to check off in the Communist-country-establishing playbook.

He thought it would be très communiste to have all the collectives not only produce food for export, but also to forge steel in their backyards. You might be thinking to yourself, "Well, I don't know much about industrializing a newly formed Communist country, but making steel girders in the backyard doesn't seem like a very good idea." That just goes to show that sometimes a little emotional distance from a situation can trump experience. It turned out to be a really bad idea.

Mao put his plan into action by having small backyard furnaces built and delivered to every collective. With their Communist zeal, stoked by Mao's great propaganda machine and some not-so-subtle threats of punishment for failure, the collectives attacked the project like they were killing a sparrow. They chanted "Long live the people's communes!" and "Strive to complete and surpass the production responsibility of 12 million tons of steel!"[3] (I'm sure the second

---

3. Erik Eckholm, "China to Let 50 Slogans Bloom (a Bit, and Just 50)," *The New York Times*, September 14, 1999, World section.

chant has a catchier ring to it in Chinese.) The collectives used all their coal to fuel the furnaces, and when they ran out of coal, they used wood. They chopped down trees, burnt their tables and chairs—they even went so far as to dig up graves to use the wood from the coffins. When iron ore wasn't available, they melted down their bicycles, their pots and pans, their shovels, hoes, and plows.

The kicker was that the girders the collectives made were useless. They didn't realize they weren't even producing steel. They were making pig iron, a weak, porous metal that needs to be refined to create steel. So the collectives were left without the basic tools needed for cooking, farming, and transportation—and with giant piles of worthless pig iron in their backyards.

This astoundingly huge miscalculation—but wait. Can you call launching a steel production campaign on a scale the world could not previously have fathomed, mobilizing the nation's entire population and dedicating to it all its resources, but never looking into how steel is actually made—can you call that merely a *miscalculation*? I say no. This egregious error, along with the drought and the agricultural disasters, resulted in chaos in the collectives as every grand plan broke down and famine set in.

The Chinese Communist Party officially called this time the "Three Years of Natural Disaster" or the "Three Years of Difficulties." As if the responsibility lay not with the CCP or Mao, but with the natural world, an unfortunate weather pattern or some other unforeseeable difficulty that came up. The peasants called it "The Bitter Years."[4]

---

4. "Different Life of Scientist Yuan Longping" (Chinese). *Guangming Daily*,

The famine-related deaths of that period are estimated to have been as high as 45 million. In Sichuan, one in seven people died. In Henan Province, one of every three people died. By 1961 the population of China had actually shrunk by 13.5 million. But the outside world would know nothing about the cataclysm of "The Great Leap Forward" for almost twenty years.

Mao's attempt to be fruitful and multiply the future and fortune of the People's Republic of China didn't result in the destruction of every living thing save for a handful of humans and a floating menagerie; still, the devastation was profound. But the meaning of that was lost on Mao. He continued to be surrounded by sycophants who reflected back his own preposterous image, and he still had tens of millions of other lives to play around with. In his mind he was just like Qin Shi Huangdi, mobilizing his people to build the Great Wall. The inevitable vulnerability of actual relationships wasn't necessary; he could continue to be the center of his empire. Perhaps the Chairman would have benefited from the transformative effect of keeping one's family together in the face of apocalyptic deluge, feeding wild beasts, shoveling their shit, and nurturing a desperate, clinging giant.

AT THE MUSEUM, Mike went outside to look at the cactus garden; I went to find the gallery I came to see. I crossed into the second cavernous building. The ceiling was over twenty feet high and the room sixty feet across. Dominating the

May 22, 2007. Accessed January 14, 2015. www.gmw.cn/content/2007-05/22/content_610656.htm (site discontinued).

far wall was a floor-to-ceiling topographical map of the Colorado River watershed, including Colorado, Utah, Arizona, Nevada, and California in the United States and Sonora and Baja California in Mexico.

The crest of the Imperial Irrigation District—a majestic crown sitting atop a shield with sunrays over a field divided diagonally by a canal flowing from a dam—sits mounted high on the wall above large, glossy pictures of various dams under the control of the district. Clearly this was the gallery with the great history of the region's water policies that the TripAdvisor review had promised me—complete with a great open space in the middle, apparently for event use. I imagined agribusiness men and women eating chicken and listening to presentations, with the giant topography of the Colorado River looming above them like an altar panel depicting the god that gives and sustains life and profit.

On the wall opposite the map was the communion of the saints, plaques of the Heroes of Old, the Men of Renown, the original families, the farmers and ranchers who came to the newly christened Imperial Valley and worked hard to figure out how to rend profit from the irrigated desert. They were men with roads named after them. On each plaque was a reproduction of each man's brand (not the kind you change your profile picture to promote—the kind you get red hot and burn into your cattle) and a few words about his character. Among them were the plaques of these nine men:

Al J. Kalin, 1888–1951. (quarter circle K)
A giant in his field . . . A man of his word
Pioneer • Cattleman • Farmer • Innovator •
Builder • Visionary

Harold Brandt, Sr., 1902–1974. (connected HL)
He settled in the Valley in 1920.
Businessman • Land Owner • Farmer • Cattleman

V. V. Williams, 1898–1984. (swinging Vs)
Co-founder of the commercial cattle feeding
industry in the Imperial Valley.
Southern Gentleman • Cattleman • Trusted Leader

Roy Westmoreland, 1886–1970. (rocking N)
Determined to win his battles in those early years.
Rugged • Generous

Harry P. Jones, 1880–1960. (T swinging V)
A true pioneer cattleman.

Ira Aten, 1862–1953. (flying A)
Linking the Old West with the New, he gave
of his best to both of them.
Lawman • Businessman • Cattleman

Alvin A. Immel, 1904–1971. (J lazy b)
Success came from drive, determination,
and the right woman.
Breeder • Cattleman • Farmer

Howard A. Foster, 1913–1994. (running H)
A cattleman's entrepreneur. He integrated
all aspects of the beef industry.
Pioneer • Philanthropist • Inventor

Edgar Carol Rutherford, 1916–1990. (crook)
He was so much for so many.
Consummate Entrepreneur

Off to the left was a smaller gallery I was looking for. It was not solely dedicated to the accidental creation of the Salton Sea, as TripAdvisor had informed me, but highlighted a part of the history of irrigating the desert. The accident was an obstacle in the fight to bring water to the barren land. There were maps and documents. There were pictures of the break in the canal, the river flooding the desert, and the attempts to fix it.

I learned that the story I had remembered and retold, while it had the broad strokes of the incident, was wrong on almost every particular. I was overwhelmed and kind of disappointed. I was overwhelmed by the legal complexities and the many personalities involved. I was disappointed that the story the exhibit chronicled wasn't more about human foolishness in attempting to bend creation to our will and ultimately how insignificant our striving is in the long arc of history. When people told me the story of the accidental creation of the Salton Sea nearly two decades earlier, I had always assumed that was their point. That it was a parable.

What I found in the Pioneers' Park Museum were the stories of land developers, entrepreneurs, farmers, and cattlemen—not existentialists. They weren't searching for grand meaning in their missteps or setbacks. Of course they didn't see themselves as Icarus flying too close to the sun; they weren't reflecting on the meaning of a breach in the wall or the great deluge stories or the complex ironies of attempting to irrigate a desert. They were pragmatists:

they wanted to develop the land, grow food, raise cattle, and make money.

For them the best part of the story wasn't their biggest mistake. It was their great success: they stopped the river. The empty room was starting to feel crowded, and I was starting to feel a little anxious, so I thought I'd take a break and look for something to buy in the gift shop.

The woman and the man behind the counter were talking casually to a gentleman who looked like he came off one of those plaques of the Great Men of Renown. He was wearing a cowboy hat and boots, but practical, not showy; his eyes were deep, and he had a stoic vibe. He seemed confident, like he was in charge of something or a lot of somethings. I wanted to talk to them. I wanted to ask them to tell me the story of the two man-made objects you can see from outer space. But instead I looked at the books on display, feeling out of place.

I'm usually anxious when I'm in unfamiliar sub-cultural territory, but I felt extra intimidated by this stoic-cowboy-man-of-renown type. I didn't know where Mike was; he had been gone a while. So there was no one in this huge museum but the four of us. It was quiet, and I thought the man and the woman and the cowboy were talking in quiet voices—or my anxiety was putting cotton in my ears; that happens sometimes. I was trying to hear what they were talking about, glancing up from the books to surreptitiously look at them, but every time I did that, the woman sort of raised her head, smiled, and opened her eyes wide, trying to make eye contact, as if to say, *Can I help you?*

Then she actually said it: "Can I help you?" Not one bit suspiciously, but in a very nice and helpful way. "We're just

chatting here. I thought you might be trying to get my attention. Are you looking for anything in particular?" All three of
them were looking at me now. I came out from behind the
book display and told them I was interested in the story of
the accidental creation of the Salton Sea. That I just wanted
to see the museum. "Oh," the man behind the counter said,
"Leanne mentioned you were coming by." I introduced myself. The stoic cowboy man was Norm Wuytens, who had
previously been a long-time curator at the museum, and the
couple behind the counter were Dean and Geneva Davidsen,
regular volunteers.

I told them my version of the Salton Sea story and asked
if they had heard it—the part about the man-made objects
you can see from outer space. Yes, of course they had. They
had heard all kinds of things. Mr. Wuytens had even heard
stories of a train engine at the bottom of the sea, swept
away in the flood, but said it wasn't true. Nor was it true
that train cars were filled with sand and run off the end of
the track into the breach to fill it up. Tracks were built up to
the break, but side-dumping cars were filled with rock, and
the rock was used as fill, not the train cars.

Mr. Wuytens said he had to go. I thanked him and then
hung around and talked to Dean and Geneva. Dean said if
I was really interested in the details, I should read *The First
Thirty Years*. The historical society had reprinted the original
1931 edition. Dean warned me that it was pretty pricey, but
I had to have it: it was remarkable, with a beautiful hard-
bound cover, carefully restored pages, and detailed contents.
The historical society had also published a limited, anno-
tated edition of *The Winning of Barbara Worth*. Geneva found
me a 1911 first edition with no dust jacket and a damaged

cover—for two dollars. It was past closing time, and I had a lot of reading to do, so we said our good-byes. After I found Mike, the two of us headed back to the Brawley Inn.

On Highway 86 we passed the Holly Sugar plant. The name has changed now, but everybody still calls it Holly Sugar. Mike worked there one miserable summer cleaning out the giant vats they used to cook down the sugar beets. It's a local landmark because there aren't any man-made structures taller in Imperial Valley. It looks like an abandoned space station on a planet no longer capable of sustaining life. Four enormous round vats, four stories high and eight times as wide, looking like steel mushroom caps, surround the central silos, the cylindrical towers reaching up to the sky. Near the top of the tallest one is a marker line under the words "Sea Level."

ONCE THE COLORADO RIVER was back to behaving the way the civilization makers and the wilderness tamers wanted it to, the construction of the canals resumed, and the irrigating of the desert was taken up with new vigor. The pioneers had fought the chaotic forces of Mother Nature and prevailed. Having broken and harnessed the river, they were eager to see what could be done about greening up the vast wasteland of the desert and putting more folks on the land.

The tussle with the Colorado River didn't seem to bring into question the wisdom of the project. Even the idea that the flooding was the result of some grand human error, that a massive miscalculation had led to the disaster, seemed to disappear. Instead, the river was recast as the enemy bent on preventing the bold visions of the Heroes of Old, the Men of Renown like Charles R. Rockwood, George Chaffey, and the men of the California Development Company who were determined to reclaim the desert.

In *The First Thirty Years, 1901–1931: Being an Account of the Principal Events in the History of the Imperial Valley, Southern California, U.S.A.*, originally published in 1931, Otis B. Tout records every possible detail from this period. He begins with the day in May 1901 when George Chaffey turned the first water into the main canal, and records every pertinent event through 1931. Tout concludes his chronicling of the conquest of the barren land with a reminder, to the reader, of its scenic beauty, finally suggesting that a visitor might enjoy driving over the newly paved roads to the Salton Sea.

Tout lays out every step that led to the break in the canal and every attempt to repair it, including the details of the financing of the project to its successful conclusion. But he isn't writing the story of the accidental creation of the Salton Sea. He's telling the story of the creation of Imperial Valley—a community of six prosperous cities, an innovative cattle industry, and the most productive farming region in the country. All built by men (and some women, no doubt) on a desert uncivilized since creation, in just thirty years. In spite of every miscalculation, lapse in reason, and failure to heed the warnings of knowledgeable men or the ancient patterns of the created environment.

Still, Tout's book is delightful to read. And in spite of its lists and tables, it's a page-turner. Tout chronicles this history with pride, counts himself lucky to have witnessed the miracle of wrestling a barren wasteland and corralling a mighty river to bring about the unimaginable. To me it seems obvious that taking a vital desert ecosystem developed over millions of years and trying to alter it in such a radical way was asking for trouble. Reading Tout's book, however, I couldn't help but get caught up in his excitement. I could almost excuse his naïveté. His generation of Men of Renown lacked the perspective that we have today, the knowledge of just how many ways it's possible to ruin the environment in a catastrophic way.

And in the end, the creation of Imperial Valley was quite an impressive feat. Every question I had about the facts of my story was answered. That's not to say that Tout and I draw the same meaning from those facts. The most surprising thing I learned was that the accidental creation of the Salton Sea, and the two-year battle to close the breach, was only one in a series of battles with the Colorado River. And as Tout and the Men of Renown saw it, the culprit wasn't primarily a profound miscalculation or poor engineering, but silt. Yes, that demon silt.

Since prehistoric times the Colorado River had been behaving like all mighty rivers do. Like the Mississippi and the Nile, it carried silt with it from the channels and canyons it carved and deposited that silt at its mouth where it met the sea, forming a vast delta. The delta region was rich in biodiversity, fruitful. Eventually the silt would build up in the delta, forming a barrier that blocked the river's outlet to the Gulf of California and turned the river waters to flood the desert. Eventually the silt would erode, and the Colorado would flow into the ocean once again. Before it was christened "Imperial" by the California Development Company, the desert was known as the Colorado Desert. The Colorado River and the Colorado Desert had a sort of yin-and-yang thing going. They worked together, complemented each other.

Silt was the problem for those Heroes of Old attempting to reverse the ten-million-year-old habits of the river. The diversion gate at the Alamo Canal would fill up with silt, and the river would go its own way. By 1905, through constant maintenance, the company was able to irrigate the land with moderate success, but that year was a wet one, which meant a bigger Colorado River and a bigger silt problem. Eventually the engineers were unable to clear it. So water stopped flowing into the canal, and the farmers and ranchers who had been persuaded by the promise of all the free water they could use were faced with dying crops and livestock.

In a desperate attempt to salvage the situation, the company's chief officer decided to make a cut into the riverbank above the canal. Bad idea. The river ran out of control through the cut, widening it and carving a deep bed as it sought the lowest ground. That point was the Salton Sink, 234 feet below sea level. Two years later it was one of only two man-made objects you could see from outer space.

There was no grandstand with a band and dignitaries pulling a lever to ceremoniously open the canal, as I had heard—or imagined. This gigantic mistake, this colossal blunder born of man's hubris, didn't occur in one dramatic moment. It happened, as is usually the case, over time, through a series of more mundane miscalculations, until things eventually got completely out of control.

President Theodore Roosevelt wasn't there, but there was a seed of truth in my memory. The company did appeal to Congress repeatedly for help, as did the Southern Pacific Railroad. The flood was destroying its tracks, and the railway had loaned the California Land Company money to help in the effort to stem the Colorado tide. President Roosevelt thought the whole project was so idiotic that he personally replied, writing a nearly 5,000-word letter, detailing the folly and flaws of the California Land Company and charging them with misconduct, acting in bad faith in order to sell land to the settlers. Roosevelt detailed the predictions by government engineers that this flooding was the result of the company's actions. He laid out how much money it would have taken from the start to accomplish the diversion of the Colorado River, charging that the company didn't have anywhere near enough capital, but that the endeavor would be so costly, it would never be worth the investment.

Roosevelt concluded his letter by saying that the flood had to be stopped and the river returned to its course for the sake of the settlers, who had been lured there under false pretense, but now were so numerous that the government had no choice but to rescue them and the company's investment. He asked the Southern Pacific Railroad to take over the project and pledged federal funds to repay the millions it would cost. The California Development Company declared bankruptcy, the railroad took over its assets, and eventually, after a two-year effort, the railroad stopped the Colorado River from filling up the desert. They were never repaid by the federal government.

In spite of the millions of wasted dollars, the intervention of the Southern Pacific Railroad, Congress, and President Roosevelt, and the bankruptcy and dissolution of the California Development Company, the whole debacle passed quickly into legend as the triumph of great men over the heartless forces of the wild.

The triumph was chronicled in newspaper and magazine articles, as well as the best-selling novel *The Winning of*

Barbara Worth by Harold Wright Bell. Otis B. Tout himself wrote a novel about the ordeal titled *Silt*. The man-made catastrophe is almost universally referred to as "the Saving of Imperial Valley" and "Reclaiming the Land." The continuing project to irrigate the Colorado Desert is known as "the Reclamation Project," which begs the question, How can one reclaim a desert? Who is it being reclaimed from? Did it once belong to investors or the government or the Heroes of Old and the Men of Renown? And who is taking it back?

Four years after the Colorado River was contained, the Imperial Irrigation District was formed to buy out the land and holdings of the California Development Company and operate the expanding system of irrigation canals and ditches, insuring that water continued to flow to the farmers. The government got behind the project on every level. In 1928 Congress passed the Boulder Canyon Project Act, which authorized the construction of the Imperial Dam, the All-American Canal, and the Hoover Dam. The Hoover Dam was built in large part to control the flooding and the silt from the Colorado River to insure that Imperial Valley wouldn't start filling up again.

CHAPTER 6

Getting Sold on Facebook . . .

S.O.S., S.O.S. . . .

"That Old Owl Put Up Quite a Fight" . . .

The Resting Place of Souls, Misguided or Otherwise . . .

Mao's "Fat Elvis" Years . . .

I have a tendency toward totalizing, infinitizing—making one thing about everything. In seconds I move fluidly from the Thai place forgetting the rice in my takeout order, to Wall Street's control of the American mind, to the general meaninglessness of life.

If someone were to ask me why I was depressed, and if they kept pressing me to the point that I had to confess that it started with forgotten rice in my takeout order—I would of course feel foolish at my over-dramatic reaction. But sometimes when I work back through my reasoning, I feel quite justified.

On a single day I heard two different segments about Facebook on public radio, one on "Morning Edition" and the other on "All Things Considered." It promised to be a day of righteous depression. When I'm in certain moods, I know it's not good for me to listen to public radio, because inevitably I'll hear a segment that will trigger my totalizing chain reaction, culminating in a generalized anger at humanity, or the hopelessness of ever stopping global warming.

The first segment was about the effectiveness of advertising on Facebook, about how companies feel like they have to advertise on Facebook because everyone is on Facebook, so if they're not advertising on it, they're not putting ads where people's eyeballs are. A friend of mine who works for a public radio station told me that success on the interwebs is all about the eyeballs, and the proof that eyeballs are on your property are the clicks on the link to your site: they click on your ad, they Like you. He also told me that if you get something for free on the interwebs, then *you* are the product. When a rad gaming site offers you free online games, they're actually offering *you* to their real customers. Or maybe they just attracted you to their site and enticed you to click on something that enabled them to jump in and just straight-up start stealing your data from you. The kicker of the NPR segment: the report concluded that advertising on Facebook was completely ineffective. That almost no one read the ads or clicked on them.

The second segment, in the afternoon, was about the Like button. About how companies feel forced to put ads on Facebook because they think that everything happens there. (So if you don't have a presence on Facebook, you have no presence at all. No one can see you.) Companies judge the effectiveness of their presence on Facebook by the number of fans their page has, and they gain fans by people Liking them.

But, early on, they discovered a problem: not very many people *liked* New Dawn dishwashing liquid or Depends undergarments or Claritin Clear decongestant or whatever it was. So a cottage industry of companies grew up that would get product Likes. Friskies cat food could just put in an order for a quarter of a million fans, and one of these little companies would get them for the Friskies folks—guaranteed. At first these Like-providing companies would get fans by paying people in Ukraine or India to "Like" Friskies, and the folks at Friskies would be self-congratulatory about the success of their foray into new media advertising. Soon these Like providers were able to dispense with paying people for Likes, because they developed robots that joined Facebook and Liked whatever their programmers told them to Like. So, Shout Stain Remover Stick ended up with 200,000 robot fans.

Similar robots are trawling dating sites and leaving comments on blogs and interacting with people to glean personal information their programmers can use to steal identities. I responded to a comment on my blog and went back and forth with the commenter several times before I realized it was a robot.

It's the triumph of the faceless on Facebook. Making connections that aren't really connections at all. How do we get back to where we meet face to face again?

I don't know what makes me feel more hopeless—the thought that millions of people are spending millions of hours online, unknowingly carrying on relationships with robots, or the thought that millions of robots are unknowingly carrying on relationships with other robots. And think of all the robot fans of New Dawn dishwashing liquid that will never take advantage of the special offers New Dawn has so cleverly targeted to them.

YEARS AGO, WHEN I first started talking about the history of the Salton Sea, my brother, Mike, sent me a bunch of slides from fishing and hunting trips my grandpa had taken there. Mike found them—in a box with a projector—on one of his visits, when he was digging through Grandpa's workshop. Mike asked if he could take the slides with him, with the promise of making prints or preserving them, and Grandpa said, Sure. He told Mike that he had started going down to the Salton Sea with some men from church. He didn't say much else. There are pictures of him standing proudly, holding up stringers of fish, from several different trips. There are posed pictures of him in front of his truck, next to some men, evidently from church, crouching down with doves that I assume he had shot, laid out, fan-like, in front of him.

In one picture he's standing with another man, and they're both holding shotguns in their right hands, barrels up. My grandpa is wearing only a wide-brimmed straw hat pushed way back on his head, brown pull-on work boots, and what he would call Jockey shorts—and I would call tighty whities. It reveals more of my grandpa than I had ever seen. The other man, about ten inches taller than him, is fully clothed, holding what looks like a dead lizard in his left hand and wearing a creepy grin. I can't tell if my grandpa is having fun. The look on his face suggests that this is a forced pose. Like this picture is meant to convince us that the hostage is there willingly, but if this were video, we could see him blinking out Morse code: S.O.S., S.O.S.

In contrast, there's a picture that must have been taken up on a rise, with the Salton Sea behind the photographer. My grandpa is squinting against the sun and holding up a stringer with two huge fish, standing on the bleached desert floor with nothing around him for what seems like miles, no break in the background except where the earth touches the sky at the horizon, the change in color barely perceptible until it grows to a pale blue at the top of the frame. You can almost feel the slight dry, hot wind.

It is unimaginable that there could be any water within a hundred miles of the place. My grandpa has a sort of mischievous grin on his face, holding these two giant fish high with his right hand and gesturing to them, palm up, with his left, as if he's just performed a magic trick, as if he's just pulled them up from the vast desert floor.

Once, Mike had put the slides in the projector and looked through them with Grandpa. When the slide show ended, Mike said that Grandpa was staring past the screen with a thin smile on his face, like he was contemplating those times, or maybe how quickly life goes by. Then he turned to Mike and said, "You know . . ." and he chuckled at whatever he was about to say, like he was seeing it in his mind. He told Mike about the time he was there fishing—and found his camper door open when he came back from the sea. He said he figured he probably didn't give it a "good shut," and as he got closer, he heard some kind of commotion inside. He set down his fishing gear and started sneaking up to the camper, still hearing this commotion, he said; he couldn't quite place the sound. When he reached the camper and pulled the door open wide—inside was this enormous great horned owl. Mike said he looked up these owls later, and they can have a wingspan of five feet and can prey on animals twice their size, like skunks and porcupines.

So this majestic predator, near the top of the food chain,

was flapping around inside the camper, knocking stuff off the little kitchen table, trying to get out. Mike told me that Grandpa paused then and smiled a kind of sore smile. "That old owl put up quite a fight. It didn't want me to get a hold of it, and all I had was this aluminum camping pan—they don't have much weight to them—so I had to hit it a couple of times to knock it down, and a half-dozen more times before it stopped moving." Then, Mike told me, he laughed, held his arms out in front of him, and said, "He got me pretty good a couple of times. Those claws are sharp." He chuckled again and shook his head, like he was thinking of good times.

When I asked Mike what he said to Grandpa, he told me, "Nothing. I didn't even know where to start."

It's hard to imagine the grandpa I knew spending a lot of time on recreation or any kind of vacation. He didn't spend money unless it was absolutely necessary, until he had tried every other way around it—he bought expired milk and dented canned goods at a discount warehouse store—so going on hunting and fishing trips, just for fun or relaxation, seemed completely unlike him. And he was never the outdoorsy type so far as I knew. I would have guessed he would have thought that hunting and fishing trips were both a waste of money and a waste of time. There was work to do. But the slides were proof otherwise.

And on one of these trips, my grandpa sat in on a sales pitch for Salton City, on the California Riviera.

When Grandpa died at ninety, in 2006, my mom saw the deed, the promise note for the Salton Sea property, in his papers. And I told her that his buying into a vacation-property scheme seemed strange, almost a little mysterious.

"No way," my mom said. "He didn't buy it for vacations—

he bought it as an investment." She went on to tell me how excited he was to get in on the ground floor. The pitch was that if the development company presold all the lots, then the bank would give them better financing, and when the lots were finished and people saw the beauty of the California Riviera, there would be an overwhelming demand. The buyers who got in on the ground floor could then purchase the lots at the locked-in price and turn around and sell them to the highest bidder.

My mom remembers Grandpa mentioning it a few more times, but she was a teenager then and interested in teenager things. A few years later the youth minister at First Baptist Church of El Cajon asked her out, and after she graduated from high school, they got married and moved to the other side of the country—to Philadelphia—so my dad could go to seminary. So my mom didn't think about my grandpa's out-of-character investment again until I started telling her about my fascination with the Salton Sea.

What made Franklin Lee Webb, who escaped the dour barrenness of the Depression era and the Dust Bowl southern plains, get pulled into buying some chance at a chance in the barren California desert? My grandpa never seemed the type to put money into something that wasn't a sure thing. He lived in El Cajon in San Diego County, a place of palm trees, beaches, and an annual average temperature of 72 degrees. What made it seem plausible to him that a paradise was being created in the desert and that he could be a part of making it happen?

But Mike and I had wanted to take a trip to the Salton Sea even before we discovered that our grandpa bought into some kind of development scheme there.

There's just something about that place: the colossal ambition of the dreams people brought there, and the tremendous ways in which they failed. Not quite comedy, but not quite tragedy, either—a sort of existential black comedy. There was something essential at our deepest core—something Mike and I suspected about ourselves—being played out in Imperial Valley. Of course, it was littered with the carcasses of ambition, striving, and the bleached bones of empire-building. But it was also the resting place of souls, misguided or otherwise, who searched for a place where they could stray from the road, slip past the barrage of cultural expectations that they live a life of predictable normalcy, and settle into a place where it was okay to be their true selves, even if they weren't yet sure who those true selves were. The desert at the Salton Sea was a place where there might just be room enough to figure that out.

MIKE IS a sculptor. He makes large-scale installations, mostly outside and out of wood. They are grand gestures that cannot survive the elements. He makes art about what he calls the Heroic/Pathetic Irony: the impulse to greatness, to do something heroic or make something important, to save someone, to change the world—coupled with the nearly simultaneous self-accusations that you're an idiot, a joke, a coward, a loser—and destined to fail.

One can ignore the accusations, dismissing them as a bit of negative thinking or temporary self-doubt, and get on with the heroism; or one can focus on each and every charge, replaying them until one is paralyzed and does nothing. It seems that most people move forward on both fronts—soldiering on while barraging themselves with disdain every step of the way. It's easy to scoff at, to ridicule the totally hubristic presumption of the Master of the Universe type, to wish failure for the Power Player. I can't help but want to ease my foot into his path and help bring about the fall, or at least the trip.

But to witness the Heroic/Pathetic dreamer, schemer, planner trip over their own feet and tumble head over heels, falling flat on their ass, elicits something else. To see someone whose gesture, from the beginning, was impossibly grand, find their inevitable failure is to see someone's soul, to recognize a fellow mis-adventurer. It is to know them in the way that you might hope to be known. The most compelling beauty is in that vulnerability. The failure of unreasonable ambitions born out of a true hunger for connection, not dominion—there's a kind of clear hope in that. In the hunger to find meaning, to be noticed or valued by someone, by God.

Is it possible that we all misunderstood my grandpa? That maybe he made a small step away from the responsibilities he was raised to shoulder toward a place that gave him the room to look for something more? To look up instead of out at the same, gradually decaying blacktop road.

WHEN JIANG QING arrived in Yan'an in 1937 to join the revolution, she started thinking seriously about finding a man she could use to climb the ranks of the Communist Party. After several affairs, she began plotting to seduce Mao. This move was bold, wildly ambitious, but she had a plan. She clapped loudly at his lectures, praised him to others in earshot of him, and probably dropped her chopsticks in the chow line in front of him and bent over slowly to pick them up. And it worked. She got herself invited back to Mao's cave for a little individual lecturing.

Shortly after their meeting, Zhou Enlai intervened. Zhou, who would become the first Premier of the People's Republic and negotiate Henry Kissinger's visit, was Mao's right-hand man—basically the guy who kept Mao's crazy in check when it came to foreign policy. One day he walked up on Mao and Jiang going at it in the bushes. Zhou, always discreet, tried to keep it on the down-low, but I expect he took Mao aside after he got his pants back on and told him he should knock it off with the young movie star. With the whole Communist revolution starting to take off, it just wasn't a good time for a scandal.

But Mao apparently didn't keep his pants on for long. Eventually other top Communist leaders found out about the affair and were scandalized. Mao was married to a woman who was a highly respected party member. She had made the Long March, which was the ultimate in old-school Communist street cred. The leaders told Mao that he couldn't disrespect someone with such deep Communist bona fides, that he must break it off with Jiang. But Mao refused. Not only would he not break it off—he was going to divorce his wife and marry Jiang. Jiang had succeeded—she had caught herself a man. You could practically hear her cackling from the bushes as he made his stand.

Members of the party pleaded with Mao to change his mind. Eventually an arrangement was made. The Party would sanction his divorce and his marriage to Jiang, but she had to agree to stay out of public politics for thirty years. "Deal!" Jiang shouted from the bushes. She became Madame Mao, and for the next thirty years she honored the agreement. And she spent that time like Max Cady in *Cape Fear*, doing knuckle pushups, studying in the prison library, and searing her white-hot plan for revenge and domination into her soul. She was making a slow but determined climb to the top of the empire.

When the sanction ran out thirty years later, the timing couldn't have been better. After the monumental disaster of the Great Leap Forward, Mao was severely criticized and resigned as head of state (though not as chairman of the Chinese Communist Party); he shifted his focus to political philosophy and poetry. Well, not completely. Mao backed his wife for the appointment as deputy director of the Central Cultural Revolution Group. From this position Madame Mao began accusing Chinese Communist Party officials of anti-revolutionary activities. Her list was made up of those who had slighted her over the previous thirty years as well as Madame and Chairman Mao's current political enemies. Mao declared that the revolution had been compromised, that capitalist sympathizers had infiltrated every level of the government and had led the culture away from the purity of the revolution. Mao oversaw the drafting of a declaration, which the Politburo passed, proclaiming the start of the Great Proletarian Cultural Revolution.

Any cultural artifact, ideology, philosophy, or individual opinion that had a connection to the West was declared anti-revolutionary and was to be destroyed or purged. Western instruments, like the piano and the violin, were destroyed. Symphonies, plays, books, art, films, puppet shows—anything with a whiff of the West was banned, burned, or outlawed. Not surprisingly, the governmental agency responsible for discovering and ruling on anti-Maoist activity as well as carrying out punishments was Madame Mao's Central Cultural Revolution Group.

When Mao was criticized for the disastrous Great Leap Forward and made to step down as head of state, the moderate Deng Xiaoping began exerting control over the governing of China. Still, even though Mao no longer controlled the day-to-day running of the country, he retained his position as chairman of the Communist Party, and people still saw him as the leader of the Revolution. He continued to produce new editions of *Quotations from Chairman Mao Tse-Tung,* popularly known as "The Little Red Book," which workers were expected to carry, memorize, and use as a guide for daily life.

In an attempt to stem the famine caused by the disastrous Leap and restore the economy, Deng and other moderates relaxed the regulation of the collectives, which allowed people to grow extra food to feed themselves and even to sell and trade. Meanwhile, Mao retreated to his palaces to refine his vision for a China that would outshine the Soviet Union and be the leading Communist power in the world.

Mao became increasingly isolated, spending most of his time in his banquet hall–sized bedroom. The windows were covered in thick drapes so that it was difficult to tell the difference between night and day. He worked and took meals in his emperor-sized bed. He had always been eccentric, but his paranoia and bizarre appetites now reached the gone-crazy zone. From 1959 until his death in 1976—these were Mao's "fat Elvis" years.

Dr. Li Zhisui, Mao's long-time personal physician, wrote a 670-page tell-all book describing Mao's abuse of sleeping pills and prescription drugs, his demands for deer-antler injections for sexual stamina, and his ceaseless and wide-ranging sexual requirements. Some pages could be laid side by side with pages from *Elvis: What Happened?* a tell-all about the King of Rock and Roll written by three of his former bodyguards. (Come to think of it, both men met Nixon around the same time, and Elvis died just ten months after Mao.) Mao tried to imitate Qin Shi Huangdi in many ways, adopting his belief that the more sexual partners he had, the longer he would live. Mao also stopped bathing, but required his guards to rub him with towels every night, concluding with a "happy ending."

While he was busy planning his immortal empire and eating the Chinese equivalent of peanut butter, banana, and bacon sandwiches in his state of sequester, Madame Mao was just stepping out into the sunshine, stretching and snapping her teeth.

Madame Mao and her three cohorts formed the Red Guard to conduct their inquisitions and mete out punishments. The Gang of Four, with Mao's backstage and semi-delusional encouragement, believed only children could be relied on to be pure Maoists. For that reason, the Red Guard was almost exclusively made up of kids. In 1966 Madame Mao ordered the military to open the armories to supply the Red Guard. Red Guard units were formed in every city and town—they were charged with rooting out anti-revolutionary behavior. The governing officials, academics, and business leaders were regularly hauled into the square and "struggled against," which meant they were beaten until they confessed to anti-revolutionary crimes. Often they were sent to work to be "re-educated" on farms. Thrown into chaos once again, the country nearly collapsed. During the Cultural Revolution, more than a million and a half people were killed, and twenty million died from disease and starvation. History still recognizes the stunning devastation wrought by the Maos' dark empire.

IF THESE HISTORIES of China seem to you, as they seem to me, almost Kafkaesque—we are not alone. Franz Kafka himself finds a complex blend of absurd striving, unchecked vanity, and a zealot's belief in technology in Qin Shi Huangdi's vision of building the Great Wall.

In his short story "The Great Wall of China," Kafka explores this dark vision. The first-person narrator, a stonemason working on one section of the Great Wall, describes a book that's all the rage at the time. Everybody working on the wall is reading it, passing it around. The book is called *The Tower of Babel*, and in it the scholar-author claims that this great tower didn't fail for the reasons everyone thinks. It didn't fail because God sent it tumbling to the ground, interpreting the people's building of the tower as arrogance or an attempt to challenge his position as ruler of the heavens. No, this writer claims that the tower collapsed because, at the time, the builders simply didn't have the technology or the skills to make the foundation strong enough to support a tower that tall. But today, the writer claims, we have the greatest stonemasons in history, the greatest engineers, the most advanced technology. And all this greatness is now coming together in the building of this Great Wall.

What is it about this book that captures the imagination of the Chinese masses? Not, says the stonemason, the claim of their technological superiority. No, what catches their attention is the speculation that the purpose of the Great Wall isn't to secure the great kingdom or to regulate its boundaries, as they have been told: the true purpose of the wall is to serve as the foundation of a new and finally achievable Tower of Babel.

Much debate surrounds the writer's claim. Some say that the Great Wall's foundation is incomplete and so is incapable of supporting a tower. Others argue that the writer's claim is meant in a more philosophical or spiritual sense. That the wall is symbolic of the people's great ability to serve as the foundation for the emperor, who is the ruler of heaven.

Were those original tower-builders a horde of arrogant sinners, challenging their creator's position? Or were they a primitive tribe lacking the skills and technology to realize the greatness they dreamed of, but trying to follow a desire God whispered in their ear at creation—to spread out, to move up? To be seen by the God in heaven who made them?

CHAPTER 7

Post-American Empire Ruin Porn . . .
Seeing China in a Haze . . .
Visiting Grandpa Webb . . .
Circumnavigating the Salton Sea . . .
Joe Stopped Speaking Chinese . . .

From the beginning, I didn't think it was a good idea, but Mike insisted, and he was driving. We found the single-engine plane behind a rusted, broken-down gas station in this apparently abandoned town on the edge of the putrid, salt-rich sea. It started up and we taxied, gaining speed. Mike pulled up quickly, before we ran out of desert ground and ended up in the sea. From the air, the ruins of the attempt at building a swinging resortland looked lonely and isolated to me. Mike didn't seem interested in my ruminations. "Watch this," he said, and did a barrel roll, then headed the plane straight toward the toxic water.

On my turn, I rode a jet ski wildly across the water until I crashed into a speedboat and plunged to the bottom. I'm not much of a gamer, but "Grand Theft Auto V" just came out, and it features a Salton Sea look-alike scenario in a place it calls the Alamo Sea. Driving around the sea and through the broken-down towns around it, I can tell that the game designers have done impeccable research. The game presents the area as a polluted wasteland of derelict buildings, surrounded by a relentless desert scattered with low-life criminals—all provided for gamers to create any kind of mayhem they like.

The Salton Sea and the remains of the California Riviera have become icons of post-American Empire ruin porn. As in Detroit, Philly, Chicago, and New Orleans, the images of structures once grand and glamorous or small and humble are alluring in deep decay. It's easy for the most amateur photographer—like me, for example—to capture striking, seemingly poignant pictures. The Salton Sea has the added folly of its creation back-story, plus the observable environmental disaster.

Today there are ruin porn websites with Salton Sea galleries. There are Pinterest boards and Instagram pages. And Googling "Salton Sea" will pull up endless images. There are the straight ruin-porn shots, and then the photo shoots using the ruins as a backdrop—for everything from weddings to ATVs. There are vacationers clowning with dead fish by the sea, and there are bands—most famously The Backstreet Boys. The Boys shot the cover of their 2013 comeback album, *In a World like This*, at the sea. It came out the week Mike and I arrived there.

Cable television also finds the Salton Sea particularly hard to resist. Anthony Bourdain visited it on his Travel Channel show "No Reservations." He had a drink with a local at the bar—The Ski Inn—in Bombay Beach. After Bourdain left, he called it an "unbelievably strange and sour place."[1]

---

1. Anthony Bourdain, "No Reservations," Travel Channel, Episode 4-15, "U.S. Southwest," August 4, 2008.

The History Channel featured the Salton Sea in two different shows, "Engineering Disasters" and "Life after People," a show dramatizing how, after people disappear from the earth, various built environments will decay.

THE GREAT WALL of China is by far the most visited ancient ruin in the world. That may be partly because it's located in a country of more than a billion people who for the most part aren't allowed to travel to any sites outside of China, but also because there's nothing else like it on earth. Nothing close to it in scale and legend. Have I mentioned that it's said to be visible from outer space?

It's easy to see why people would visit the ruins of something once magnificent like the Great Wall. But what motivates people to visit the decaying ruins of an unfinished, ill-conceived, and hardly unique vacation resort on the shores of an increasingly toxic, accidentally created sea in the middle of the desert? Sure, the sea is also said to be visible from outer space, but the fading motel marquees and windowless, moldering trailer homes are barely visible from the highway. In most of the popular-culture coverage of the Salton Sea Riviera, there is a reviling tone suggesting the moral failure of its creators and inhabitants. It's as if all this decay is the deserved consequence of a depraved citizenry.

But not everyone who documents the Salton Sea today views the ruins as shorthand for moral decay. Kim Stringfellow, an artist and educator, documents the decay of built environments and creates exhibitions that draw people into dialogue with the subject matter. And the 2006 documentary *Plagues & Pleasures on the Salton Sea* by filmmakers Chris Metzler and Jeff Springer has all the ruin "money shots," but also explores the area's communities and the people who live there. In the ten years since the film debuted, the filmmakers have continued to work to bring attention to the people and plight of the Salton Sea.

Are we a long way from Genesis here, from God's commanding humans to spread out and up? Or do we see in the devastation of the Salton Sea a faint imprint of the ruins of the Tower of Babel? Is this the consequence of reaching too far, too high? It's something that this small world's creators never could have imagined. Something that Mildred de Stanley, rhapsodizing in the 1960s about this heavenly resort, couldn't possibly have foreseen.

XI JINPING, the current president of the People's Republic of China, is one of the Crown Prince Party, an unofficial group of politicians whose parents established the Chinese Communist Party and the country. He was born four years after the birth of the People's Republic of China, and at age fourteen answered the call from Madame Mao and the Gang of Four to young people to purify the revolution. He joined the Red Army and became a young leader in the revolution. After Mao died and the Gang of Four were arrested, he quickly distanced himself from involvement with them.

Xi Jinping skillfully worked his way up the government ladder, eventually becoming the supreme leader of China in 2013. Five days later, my Gang of Four—the band—played at Yugong Yishan, a rock club in a trendy district of Beijing. The reviews were generally positive—except for the ventilation system. Without a good ventilating system in a crowded rock club, the atmosphere can quickly become unbearable.

Poor air quality in China, especially in the major cities

and manufacturing districts, makes it dangerous to breathe. Recently, after a long stretch of extremely bad air-pollution days, President Xi took a stroll—without a mask—through the same trendy neighborhood where the Gang of Four played, attempting to reassure people it was safe.

But this reassurance was simply propaganda: the air pollution in Beijing is real. It's not only unhealthy for residents; it's also unhealthy for tourists—and for the economy. When the air quality is really bad, people stay inside; they don't go to restaurants, shops, or tourist attractions, and they don't spend money. During the stretch that brought President Xi out for his mask-less stroll, visits to the Forbidden City, the most popular tourist attraction, were down to one-quarter of the daily average. The official media praised the president for coming out to breathe with the people and demonstrate that there was no need for smog-panic, even as *The Guardian* website reported that Chinese scientists warn that Beijing is dangerously close to being uninhabitable. The thick, dark smog is so dense that only about 50 percent of the usual amount of sunlight is able to penetrate it, with a noticeable effect on plants' ability to photosynthesize. No wonder people can hardly catch their breath in the city.

MY GRANDPA ONLY ever gave me two things: one is his Union Worker Study Bible, and the other is a Thirty-Aught-Six rifle.

The Union Worker Study Bible I found in his workshop when I stopped to visit him once on my Christmas break from seminary in Berkeley. There was a routine to visiting my grandpa. I would pull into the dirt driveway, past a little eucalyptus grove, the dog would start barking, and I would sit in the car until he came out of the house, wiping his mouth with the back of his hand or wiping his hands with a handkerchief, like he hadn't been expecting anyone and was caught in the middle of eating or working. A big, slow grin would spread across his face as he walked toward the gate, and he would say something like, "Well, look who it is." Like I had just showed up out of the blue. Then he would tell me where to park my car: "Pull in there next to the truck" or "Put it right in back of Grandma's Chrysler. She's not going anywhere—she already got her hair done." As I parked the car, Grandpa would mosey toward me. Grandpa moved slow not because he was old and weak—he was actually strong and sure—but because that was his way. Maybe it was the way of his Missouri people.

We would go inside and sit in the living room for a bit. He would ask a few questions about my brothers and my sister, make a half-joking comment about Berkeley being Sodom or Gomorrah, he couldn't remember which one, and I would make a comment about how the dog—or the cat or the bird—really must be getting old. Then, after a pause, he would get up out of his chair and say, "Well, I guess we better have a look around."

This was my favorite part of any visit. We would go out through the kitchen, where he would say to my grandma, "Mother, we're gonna go walk a bit." We would head into the breezeway, where there was a table with a few old hats among pruning shears, work gloves, old glass bottles, and plants he was starting. He would pick up a greasy, well-worn feed cap, knock the dust off it with a slap to his thigh, and hand it to me: "You better put this on." I would take it and nod: Yeeee-up. Then he would pick up his hat, brushing off the brim before putting it on. I assumed the hat was for the sun, but it wasn't always sunny.

And, like we always did when I visited him, we would go out to walk the land. That meant walking around his property and sort of surveying the place. He would show me new vegetables or flowers he had planted or point out how a particular tree was coming along or how a repair was holding up. I always assumed this routine was a holdover from generations of Missouri farmers. It was just what you did every day to keep an eye on things. I don't know how big a farm he grew up on, but the land we walked in El Cajon was one acre. When my Grandpa bought it in 1949, it was way out in the country, but by the 1990s it was just a semi-crappy suburb of San Diego.

Walking the land, we would always end up in his workshop. It was the first thing my grandpa built when he bought the land, before he and his family even moved onto it. He built the workshop, then an outhouse. Then he bought a small trailer and moved my grandma and their three daughters—my then twelve-year-old mom and her two little sisters—from the rented house in Ocean Beach into the trailer. Next he built the garage, moved the family in there, sold the trailer, and started working on the house. He was building something of his own. Maybe not irrigating a desert, or establishing a new country, or building an empire, but he was making something all his own.

The workshop was like an old barn with a shack attached to it. There were rooms full of things he was planning on fixing one day or that he couldn't bear to get rid of, because you never know what you might need. That particular visit, while he was showing me a drawer full of broken, rusty harmonicas and leather-working tools, I noticed a book wrapped in plastic on the shelf above the workbench. "What's that?" I asked. He looked at it, paused, and then took it down from the shelf. He started unwrapping it before he started speaking. "This . . ."—he pulled it free of the plastic, took out his handkerchief and wiped it down on all sides, and held it out to me, laying it flat on the palm of his hand—". . . is the Bible that was given to me when I first got out here."

I picked it up and read the printed cover: *The Union Study Bible*. I paged through it, and it appeared to be just that—there were verses highlighted with notes about brotherhood and labor and laborers and God blessing the work of our hands. There were passages underlined in pencil, with notes written in the margins. I would have guessed my grandpa was in a union because he worked in an airplane factory, but as long as I was old enough to understand terms like "liberal" and "conservative," I knew my grandpa to be an over-the-top, right-wing Republican. He proudly displayed a picture of Ronald Reagan on his mantle. I don't know what was more shocking to imagine—that my grandpa used to go to union Bible studies, or that unions used to have Bible studies.

"Would you like to have that?" he asked, his voice quieter than usual. I would, I told him. He turned his head to one side and nodded; then he handed me the plastic wrapping.

The Thirty-Aught-Six rifle just came in the mail one day. I knew so little about guns or gun-owning that when the long, rectangular box came for me with my grandpa's return address on it, I couldn't imagine what was in it. I opened it, and there was the gun, without note or explanation.

I called my brother Mike. "Guess what I just got in the mail from Grandpa?"

"A gun? Yeah, I got one too. So did Matt and Dad."

Evidently, my grandpa had read in some fundamentalist Christian, pro-militia version of the *National Enquirer* that the state of California planned to start going door to door collecting people's guns, so he mailed them out of state, one to his son-in-law and one to each of his grandsons, for safekeeping.

My grandpa was a peaceful man, but he wanted to keep the peace on the land he had worked so hard to make his own. So he had his fence and his dog—and his firearms, if it came to that. He had spread out and been fruitful on that land, and he wanted to keep his home and his family secure. In the end, he just wanted to protect his dreams.

CENTURIES BEFORE, Qin Shi Huangdi had a dream of protecting his united empire with a great wall. But this big dream, like so many, had a dark side that made history. All the arduous planning and building it took to realize his vision required unending sacrifice by the peasant masses. According to numerous accounts, they died by the hundreds of thousands during the Wall's construction, and many of them were buried inside the Wall itself. Not surprisingly, for most of China's history, the Wall has been a symbol of oppression and the unchecked demands of the powerful on the majority peasant population.

Qin could never have imagined this damning legacy—or the rise and fall of his wall's greatness. During the Ming Dynasty 1,200 years later, the building of the Wall reached the height of human ambition as the structure grew in both size and grandiosity. But the times both before and after were marked by numerous periods when the Wall's symbolic and architectural prowess was impeached.

In the Chinese language that Qin standardized, the Wall's adjective means "long," though it is historically translated as "great" in English. Subsequent dynasties, whether they maintained the Wall, expanded it, or ignored it, refused to use Qin's name for it to avoid being associated with his reputation as the great oppressor.

The lesson, whether ancient or recent, is the same. The bold visions of the Men of Renown, whether they create monuments or missteps or both, usually end up costing most to those who can afford it least.

MIKE AND I wanted to make our own post-American Empire tour. So we decided to circumnavigate the Salton Sea in my 2006 Prius. Starting in Brawley, we would take Highway 78 out of town, cut over to Kalin Road, and go to the south end of the sea to visit the Sony Bono Wildlife Refuge. Then we'd head 65 miles up Highway 111 on the east side and 65 miles back down Highway 86 on the west side, stopping at cities, towns, beaches, campgrounds—anything we felt called to explore.

Before we started out, we met Al Kalin Jr. for coffee at the Aspen in the Desert Restaurant, conveniently located across the parking lot from our room at the Brawley Inn. Al Kalin Jr. knows a lot about a lot of things. He's the son of one of the original Heroes of Old: his father has a plaque on the wall of the Imperial County Historical Society and, of course, has a road named after him.

Al's father came to Imperial Valley in 1915 and established the cattle industry there. When Albert Kalin Sr. died, his wife, Louise Kalin, took over the cattle feedlot and the 3,000-acre farm and the innovative agricultural business, in addition to raising Al and his younger brother. When Al was six, his mother added to their land holdings, buying eighty acres on the south end of the Salton Sea, near where the New River enters the sea. Until 1999, Mexicali factories and manufacturing plants dumped all kinds of discharge and waste directly into the river. A Mattel toy factory in Mexicali regularly dumped rejected toys into it. As a boy, Al remembers finding deformed green army men washing up all over the shore.

At California Polytechnic State University in San Luis Obispo, Al studied crop science, soil science, agricultural engineering, and game bird management. Now he's both an innovative farmer and a passionate environmentalist. He's also a member of the Outdoor Writers Association of California, contributing a regular outdoor column to the local newspaper. His love of fishing led him to develop a line of fishing lures that became increasingly popular: at one point nearly 30 percent of all tackle boxes had a Kalin's lure in it. When he was awarded Farmer of the Year in 2013 by the Imperial Valley Farm Bureau, the executive director concluded her remarks by saying, "In reality, Al Kalin is nothing short of a Renaissance man in muddy boots."[2] There's probably no one who knows more about the Salton Sea than he does. He knows the history, the science, and the politics.

Al was already seated in a booth by the front window with an iced tea when Mike and I arrived. He was wearing a feed cap and a button-down shirt. He had kind eyes and a patient smile. The day before, when I called his cell phone

---

2. "Al Kalin: 2013 Farmer of the Year," Imperial County Farm Bureau; see www.icfb.net/foy_2013.html. Accessed July 2013.

out of the blue and asked if I could interview him about the Salton Sea, he simply said yes, and suggested we meet the next morning.

When my brother and I sat down in the booth, I let a question stumble out of my mouth—I was just getting my bearings, opening my Moleskine, writing the date and the word "Interview" across the top of the page and then underlining it. Al began answering the question he figured I was trying to ask, because what I actually said was something like, "How long have you known the Salton Sea?" That was when he told the story about the deformed army men washing up on the shore.

Then he covered more recent history. "About five years ago the U.S. built an 84-million-dollar water treatment plant on the Mexico side of the border. Some sewage still comes in, but all the pathogens are gone. But with the water now clean enough to use for farming, Mexico diverts some, so about 25 percent less water is flowing into the Salton Sea each year from the New River."[3]

Al is also the Imperial County Farm Bureau's On-Farm TMDL Consultant. (TMDL, Total Maximum Daily Load refers to the maximum amount of a pollutant a body of water can take in daily and still meet regulation safety levels.) So he knows about pathogens and silt. Remember Otis B. Tout and the demon silt? Silt carries the chemicals from the fertilizers used in the tens of thousands of acres of farmland. Al developed a system that has greatly reduced the agricultural runoff into the Salton Sea, an achievement that won the bureau the Governor's Environmental and Economic

---

3. Al Kalin, discussion with the author, July 2013.

Leadership Award, and the Environmental Protection Agency's Environmental Award for Outstanding Achievement.

Al explained that the fertilizer runoff that flows into the Salton Sea causes massive algae blooms, which die and sink to the sea bottom. When the algae breaks down, it produces hydrogen sulfide, which robs the water of oxygen and causes that terrible stench. "I thought the smell was from all the dead fish," I said.

"Hydrogen sulfide creates dead zones in the sea where there isn't enough oxygen," Al explained, "and that kills everything that needs oxygen—fish and barnacles. The fish kills add to the smell. I live at the south end of the sea, and before we put this program into place, the stench was so bad, we always had to light candles in the house."[4]

Al went on to explain more of the history, science, and politics of the looming environmental disaster.

When he finished, I said, "Knowing what's coming and knowing what has brought us here, do you think it would have been better if the irrigation canals had never been built? Do you think farming in Imperial Valley shouldn't have started in the first place?" Then I asked what I thought was the obvious conclusion: "Do you think irrigating the desert was a bad idea?"

Al smiled quickly, sat back a little, and folded his hands together, resting them on the table. Looking at them and then at me, he said, "That's like asking me what I think of my dog."[5]

I wasn't quite sure what Al meant by that, but it seemed

---

4. Al Kalin, discussion with the author, July 2013.
5. Al Kalin, discussion with the author, July 2013.

important. It seemed poignant. Like the connection, the bond was too strong to be broken.

WHEN JEANNE, MARIA, JOE, and I stepped out of the hotel onto the sidewalk in central Beijing, the air was visible, a classic London fog, a real pea-souper, only with less romance and a dark vibe—sort of a shaving-years-off-our-life-expectancy vibe. The pain we were feeling in our throats and chests came simply from breathing the air. I didn't have a mask—I never imagined I would need one—and I didn't have masks for my wife or kids, either. So we went back inside the hotel to wait for our car. We were nearing the end of our travels; we had saved our visit to the Great Wall to bring our experience of China to a close, to punctuate our trip.

Okay, it wasn't saved to punctuate—I'm not even sure what sort of punctuation it would have been. At this point in the trip, I was incapable of any sort of meaningful gesture. China had beaten any pretense out of me, left me incapable of self-reflection or recontextualization of my experiences. All I was able to do was focus on meeting the basic needs of my wife and children—finding food and water, guiding them through the pressing crowds, keeping everyone together and moving forward.

There are just so many people in China.

I know that's an incredibly obvious comment to make—and it's the one fact everybody from Muscatine, Iowa, to Holtville, California, knows about China. But it's one thing to have absorbed a cultural awareness of this, and a very different thing to be living with it—in the constant throng, crowded, pushed, and bumped. I always felt sticky or itchy.

Joe stopped speaking Chinese because every time he did, in a store or on the street, people were so amazed to see a little white boy speaking their language that they called out to everyone around them. All of them wanted to talk to him and touch him. Once I had to pull him out of a crowd of uniformed school kids after he had been signing autographs for fifteen minutes. At first he thought it was fun, but when he started looking scared, I got him out of there.

I had assumed that after we arrived in the more cosmopolitan international cities, the conditions would be better, but they remained unrelenting—with the exception of a brief three-day respite visiting our friends Ben and Jodi in Shanghai.

They lived in a walled, guarded compound. And once we walked through the gates, China disappeared. There were tree-lined streets, row houses, driveways, yards, a central pool and bar. It was like heaven. Ben grilled steaks in the backyard, and we listened to the local radio station from back home and talked. My family and I washed all our clothes and bathed several times in a row until a familiar soap smell returned to our hair and our underwear.

Like so many other foreigners, Ben was there representing the manufacturing interests of a company from his native country. Shanghai is where business is done. In fact, Shanghai has a long history as an international city. In the 1930s, it was a Jazz Age mecca, rich with music, nightclubs, cinema, arts and literature. The British, Americans, and especially the French had a large presence there.

This is the Shanghai where Jiang Qing—Madame Mao—became a movie star. It is this history, however, that kept Shanghai out of the running for the earliest economic reforms. When, after Mao's death, Deng Xiaoping assumed control of the country and instituted his "capitalism with Chinese characteristics," he was distrustful of Shanghai's past connections with the West. Deng preferred to build something out of nothing on the barren plains of Shenzhen, so he could control it from the ground up.

But "capitalism with Chinese characteristics" quickly began to look like just plain old capitalism. It echoed the dissolution of the Soviet Union and capitalist reforms in Russia: those in power got rich, and the people under them still worked hard with little to show for it. It was the rapid economic reform without any political reform that led, in part, to the Pro-Democracy Movement in 1989. It was a kind of bizarre Cultural Revolution: instead of pitting themselves against other groups in the Communist empire, the students leading the movement invited the intellectuals, workers, and merchants to join them. They all came together to demand "a Communist Party without corruption."

Anti-government protests erupted throughout China, the largest being in Tiananmen Square, under the gaze of Mao's portrait. The demonstration in the square grew: students came from all over the country to join in, and police, soldiers, and low-level Party officials joined in as well. At this point the Politburo declared martial law and brought in troops from outlying regions. Deng then insisted that to restore order to the capital, the square must be cleared. So troops marched in and opened fire.

The government's official position is that no blood was shed in Tiananmen Square. Deng, in a speech he gave three days after the massacre, asked rhetorically, "What? Do you think our People's Liberation Army soldiers would do such a thing? Was Tiananmen washed in blood? Of course not!" Which was a calculated face-saving response, since the Red Cross had immediately reported 2,600 deaths in the square. (After Deng's speech, it withdrew its report.) A U.S. State Department report claims that most of the deaths took place on the roads outside the square, where people were shot as they were fleeing.

Jeanne was in China at the time, teaching English in Harbin in the north. Most American teachers were evacuated when the protests began, but Jeanne was on her own and had no one to evacuate her, so she stayed through the turmoil. When Jeanne and her friends from that time talk about the massacre, they say, using finger quotes, "hundreds if not thousands dead," which even today seems to be as specific as anyone is officially willing to be.

There were no cell-phone videos or tweets to counter the official story, but there were enough foreign reporters to put out some images and information. Enough so that the World Bank suspended its loans to China, and foreign investment and joint ventures were canceled. Just as Deng's dreams of China as a leading world economy were gaining momentum, the world's response to the suppression of the Pro-Democracy Movement and the Tiananmen Square massacre was set to destroy them.

In a gesture to show the world that corrective action was being taken, Deng Xiaoping resigned. Jiang Zemin, the party secretary of Shanghai, replaced him. In an effort to win the world back, President Jiang opened Shanghai to foreign investment and applied broad economic reforms to entice corporations to set up shop and take advantage of the astronomically low labor costs and sparse regulations. Just twenty-five years later, the population has doubled to more than 26 million, making it the largest city in the world. During that time it has become one of the world's most important financial centers, with the world's fifth-largest stock exchange.

THE IMPULSE WHISPERED in Adam's ear at creation—for me it explains the Great Wall, the Salton Sea, and so much more. Why move forward? Why court failure by trying to make big dreams come true? Why does anyone want to grow, to be the best, to succeed? It's not a decision—it's a compulsion, contradictory as it may seem, imbedded in us by our Creator.

THE FIRST ATTEMPT to repurpose the 525-square-mile gaffe called the Salton Sea? Turn it into a sports-fishing mecca. I learned this while reading the chapter titled "Fishing" in Mildred de Stanley's book on the Salton Sea. She records a nearly year-by-year history, beginning in 1929, of the attempts by the California Department of Fish and Game to stock the Salton Sea and the subsequent results.

In 1929 and 1930, the striped bass was transplanted from both the San Joaquin River and the San Francisco Bay. The ghost shrimp, the mudsucker, and the pile worm were also introduced as food for the striped bass. But the bass didn't survive. While the intended predator failed to thrive, the pile worm established itself as potential food for any future species of game fish. Within two years, the three-inch-long water worms numbered in the billions.

In 1934, 15,000 silver salmon were stocked in the Salton Sea, but they went the way of the striped bass. In 1948, anchovies from the Gulf of California and Alamitos Bay in Mexico were brought in by plane to establish a population of small-sized fish that would serve as food for larger game fish. But they too failed to thrive.

In 1950, the Department of Fish and Game decided to take every species that they could net out of the Gulf of California, put them on trucks, drive them the 200 miles to the Salton Sea, release them, and see what took. Species introduced included the corvina, the gulf croaker, the pompano, the halibut, white and silver perch, bonefish, smelt, pex del rey, the mojarra, the grunion, anchovies, anchovettas, sardines, and the totuava. Also introduced were one species of squid, four kinds of clams, three kinds of mussels, and two kinds of oysters. The grand result: None of them were known to survive in the Salton Sea—except the corvina.

Yes, finally, a champion, a game fish suited for an inland salt-water sea, 234 feet below sea level, on an active fault line, fed by agricultural runoff, with a water temperature reaching a high of 95 degrees. There was just one small catch: the corvina proved hard to—well, catch.

Despite these dispiriting results, the Department of Fish and Game kept at it, engaging biologists and conservationists and commissioning a three-year study by the University of California at Los Angeles, all the while continuing to try to get other species to flourish in the Salton Sea. After all, what's the use of having a giant, man-made sea in the middle of the desert if you can't scoop fish and other creatures out of their natural habitat in the ocean and make them live in those accidental waters? The UCLA study found some positive proof: the gulf croaker, a small fish, had actually survived the massive catch-and-release of 1950. A small population of them was feeding off the pile worms, and the croakers were then being eaten by corvina.[6] Bless those little pile worms' hearts—they had been waiting twenty years to get a little food-chain started, and now things seemed to be taking off.

But corvina were still tricky to land. There were reports that they were being caught with shrimp bait off the docks at the U.S. naval air base on the south shore. A warning was issued, however: the top-secret base was closed to unauthorized personnel, and anyone entering the area was endangering their life. You really had to want to catch a fish.

This base was also used to test which shapes would work best for the atomic bomb. In 1944 there were over 150 prototypes dropped at the Salton Sea. The *Enola Gay* made secret flights from its base in Utah so the crew could practice its aim before heading to Japan. The base was also used to test parachutes for capsules for the manned space program, which leads me to wonder: Could the astronauts see this base from outer space?

Eventually, someone figured out how to catch the abundant but elusive corvina (a four-inch wobbling-spoon lure did the trick), and then it wasn't hard for the casual angler to catch their limit. The best time to land corvina was at the height of summer, when the water at the bottom of the Salton Sea didn't contain enough oxygen because of decaying organic matter. That would drive corvina up to shallower water so they could breathe, and that's when anglers (like my grandpa?) could really haul them in. But that same process

---

6. Mildred de Stanley, "Fishing," in *The Salton Sea: Yesterday and Today* (Los Angeles, CA: Triumph Press, 1966).

also caused large annual die-offs of the smaller fish, which lined the shores by the stinking millions.

In 1965, an apparent accident at a tropical fish farm introduced mollies to the Salton Sea. The small fish, raised to sell at pet shops, were swept away in a flash flood and ended up there. The mollies quickly became the most populous species.

All those years of work. All the scooping and hauling and flying fish in. All the planning and directing. And, in the end, an accidental flood and a pet-store fish do the trick.

SO MANY TALES of ambition and ruin. . . . Franz Kafka wrestled with the Tower of Babel in at least four stories or parables. "Had it been possible to build the tower without ascending it," he wrote, "the work would have been permitted." But people's desire to reach up to God, or for God, beyond their earthbound selves, is the same desire, action, or trajectory—is the very impulse to continue creation in the way that God had commanded them.

According to Kafka, it wasn't the great technological achievement of the tower that displeased God, but the ideas that the people had about themselves when they stood at the top of the tower, reaching up to the heavens, and looked out over the whole earth. The people were looking down on the world from space, from God's point of view. It was heady stuff. Did it change them somehow? To look down from God's perspective?

What goes up must come down. This is the law of gravity and of the human psycho-spiritual sense of the self. There is something deeply integral to the makeup of the human species that compels us to create something beyond what we have previously experienced, to imagine something that doesn't exist, which seems to produce as a byproduct a kind of flush of power—like a toxin in the blood or the soul, a toxin that distorts our desire to further creation, twisting it into a claim of authorship. As if we have the power to make the world.

CHAPTER 8

The Glamour Capital of the Salton Sea . . .

The Assuredness of Future Growth . . .

Chairman Mao and His Madame . . .

The New Recreation Capital of the World . . .

The Only Fish Found in the Salton Sea . . .

In 1958 in Imperial Valley, at least four major developers laid out plans for the resort cities of the future, all including motels, restaurants, elaborate marinas, and yacht clubs. But plans were also made for decidedly downscale developments, trailer home parks, and even resort campgrounds. There was an opportunity for every size dream.

At Salton Sea Beach, a small store started by long-time resident Helen Burns, on her return from college in 1947, was being transformed. Her first customers were illegal immigrants looking for work on Imperial Valley farms; eventually, the slowly growing number of anglers discovered the store. But when the investment craze hit the sea in 1958, she made over her little store in a big way: it became Helen's Beach House Resort and Marina, with a restaurant, cocktail lounge, motel, and trailer park.

Other cities and businesses that had been sweating it out in the desert for years also worked to get in on the action. Niland and Bombay Beach put in marinas, and the

Hot Springs were remodeled and expanded. The Fountain of Youth Hot Springs went from a smattering of small huts around the naturally occurring springs to a full-service luxury health spa and resort.

The most breathtaking audacity was shown by the men who proposed to set out whole new cities on the desert sand, creating out of nothing the landscape where lives would be lived. Mr. Ray Ryan, who is by turns described as a land developer, an oilman, and a professional gambler, chose a spot on the northeast shore off Highway 111.[1] Ryan's plans for North Shore Beach Estates included the North Shore Motel, the North Shore Marina, several modern restaurants, and Ryan's crown jewel: the members-only North Shore Beach and Yacht Club.

The clubhouse was designed by modernist architect Albert Frey, who is remembered as the father of Desert Modernism. This very regional style is found in the southern California deserts, but primarily in Palm Springs and the area extending slightly south to the north shore of the Salton Sea. The style takes its cues from the Bauhaus school and adapts them for the extreme environments of sun and sand, giving structures wide overhangs, dramatic roof lines, outdoor living spaces, and a lot of metal, glass, and concrete.

At the Salton Sea, Frey was asked to design entire developments, the first being Ray Ryan's great venture. The North Shore Yacht Club, which cost two million dollars, was designed to resemble a ship just breaking the waters of the

---

1. H. Marynell, "Ray Ryan—Life as a Gamble," *Hacienda Hot Springs*. Accessed June 8, 2016.

Salton Sea, complete with catwalks, a flying bridge, masts, flags, and portholes.

An early promotional sales film gives a glimpse into what was already being called "The Glamour Capital of the Salton Sea."[2] The camera pans across the completed clubhouse and marina, taking the prospective investor on tour, as the narrator, with a voice somewhere between astonishment and gratitude, explains the wonders unfolding. After initial shots of the yacht club's ship-like exterior and the 400-boat marina, showing several boats at anchor, the film focuses on the landing strip, which, as the narrator explains, will soon be replaced by a fully modern skyport.

In addition to the marina and clubhouse, the development includes the less dramatic but still desirable North Shore Motel. Adjacent to the motel is the Youth Village, where young people can have fun in the sun and can play both shuffleboard *and* ping-pong. And all of this, the narrator points out, is at the disposal of investors and lot owners in the exclusive residential community of North Shore Estates.

Across the sea, on the west shore, development was keeping pace. Brothers Boyd and James Thomas began work on Desert Shores—"Shores" being the operative word. They carved up the shoreline into ten long fingers jutting out into the sea to create thirteen miles of coastline. A road ran down the middle of each finger, there were fifty lots per finger, and each lot had its own dock. With the addition of the Desert Shores Yacht Club and ready-to-build lots laid out for

---

2. *Past Pleasures at the Salton Sea: A Collection of Films, Photos, & Music from the Glory Days of the Salton Sea.* Tilapia Film, 2008.

hundreds of new homes, serviced with paved streets, water, sewer, and electrical, Desert Shores was poised for the inevitable flood of buyers to the Jewel of the Salton Sea.

If that sounds familiar, it's no wonder—almost every development used the same descriptive phrase. At some point, every development and new project—in its promotional films, flyers, and newspaper ads and brochures—referred to itself as not only the Jewel of the Salton Sea, but also the Center of the Desert Empire, the Queen of California's Vacation Empire, the Heart of the Salton Riviera—with additional adjective/noun combinations suggesting exotic, regal locales.

The optimism could be read on the street signs of Desert Shores' yet-to-be-inhabited neighborhoods: Capri Lane, Marseille Lane, Venice Lane, Honolulu Lane, Acapulco Lane; and Malibu, Monterey, and Redondo, among others. The main street, double wide and lined with palm trees, was named Desert Shore Drive. From the entrance on Highway 86, it ran right through the middle of town and straight to the marina and the yacht club.

Desert Shores, while impressive in its pretention, wasn't the most ambitious enterprise in 1958. For the true Queen of the California Riviera, head twelve miles south to Salton City. In May of that year, M. Penn Phillips, the dean of American land developers, laid out the plans for a city that would rival Palm Springs in population, amenities, and character. As Mildred de Stanley explains in her worshipful book, "Salton City was a planned community, planned for orderly growth to avoid the chaotic conditions that are so prevalent in other cities in Southern California. They had an intelligent master plan, with provisions for churches, schools, parks, recreational areas, residential family areas, multi-family areas, and commercial areas."[3]

Land surveyors marked off 250 miles of road, 25,000 residential lots, commercial and civic plots, as well as the marina and yacht club—all designed by Albert Frey.

When Mike and I were there, I read the street signs to get a glimpse of what the developers were envisioning, what sort of houses, landscaping, cars in the driveway. And ultimately, what sort of people they imagined would replace the little plastic figures on their architects' models when they went full-scale. In developments like these, the street names were created for the buyers—another sales pitch.

Salton City's street names follow the themes of majestic sun and majestic sea and then just other majestic or fancy things. Apparently it was difficult to come up with numerous street names around a given theme. Either through exhaustion or exasperation, the name-makers went off the rails, with some of the names not following the developer's theme or making any particular sense for the community. I always imagine that the street-naming was given, as a small gesture, to the developers' spouses or children.

I'm guessing that the small cluster of street names referencing elite universities was a wife's doing. In a little southwest tangle of cul-de-sacs there are Berkeley, Stanford, Dartmouth, Vassar, and Harvard Avenues. There is also a small cluster of planet names with a few constellations thrown in: Uranus, Venus, Mercury, and Mars Avenues, and Big Dipper Drive.

Not surprisingly, there's also a sand cluster: Sand Crest,

---

3. Mildred de Stanley, *The Salton Sea: Yesterday and Today* (Los Angeles, CA: Triumph Press, 1966), p. 62.

Sand Jewel, Sand Ranch, Sand Flower, Sand Quail, Sand Hill, Sand Man, and Sand Ere Avenues. Sand Ranch and Sand Hill don't exactly conjure images of grandeur, but Sand Ere is an interesting choice. It is clearly the old English word meaning "before" that is intended, not the more common word it suggests, meaning "mistake." Although I'm not clear what might be meant by "sand before." It could just be a literal statement about what the street was before it existed.

Moving north towards S. Marina Dr., the sand gives way to shore: Shore Island, Shore Rock, Shore King, Shore Gem, Shore Breeze, and on and on. Until Seashore Avenue, where the dominant naming theme plays out to near-exhaustion. The word "sea" is coupled with nouns from the expected to, I would say, the unexpectedly intriguing. The more obvious names include Seagull, Seaport, Seashore, Sea View, Sea Life, Sea Oasis, and Sea Wind Avenues. Then the names venture a bit further out with Sea Kist, Sea Garden, Sea Raider, and, yes, Sea Elf.

De Stanley reports that by 1961, water and sewer lines were complete; she estimates that the system was capable of serving a population of 40,000. The Salton Bay Yacht Club was open, with a restaurant, bar, and banquet facilities where 300 people could enjoy the seaside view from the club's unique, two-story circular design. In addition to the yacht club, there was the Salton Bay Motor Hotel, an eighteen-hole golf course, and an airport open to the public. De Stanley concludes, "With Salton City as the entrance to this vast vacation area, as well as its own attractions, the growth of the city seems assured."[4]

---

4. de Stanley, *The Salton Sea*, p. 67.

That assuredness of the future growth of the area surrounding the Salton Sea, and the prosperity of its new resort cities in particular, was as abundant as the saltwater and the desert sand on which they would be built. Which was fortunate, because, as it turns out, it wasn't primarily the land that the developers were selling—it was that certainty in the growth, that confidence in the inevitability of the unimaginable return on investments.

It was the same empire-out-of-sand story sold by the California Development Company when they promised unending prosperity and free water to everyone willing to move to the desert and put their money down. It was the same story sold by Qin Shi Huangdi, who promised an eternal kingdom of peace and unity if his people were willing to make sacrifices (sometimes their lives) for the mighty emperor's vision of building a wall so great it would thwart all would-be marauders. It is the same story we read in Genesis, the story about how we can make a great name for ourselves if we spread out and up, if we all work together to build a great tower that reaches toward heaven.

IN 1937 THE JAPANESE occupied Shanghai and took over the Chinese film industry. Jiang Qing fled to Yan'an, where Mao and the other leaders were waging the revolution from caves carved into the mountainsides. Mao was twenty-one years older than Jiang when they met. From this point began the gestation of the villainous, white-boned demon (what the Chinese called her after her downfall). A gestation that would last thirty years, until she was born, fully formed, as a vengeful sociopath, consuming her young and destroying millions of faceless peasants through her delusional policies and real or perceived enemies in an unquenchable desire for power.

I know—that sounds a little over the top. But it's the kind of melodramatic vitriol that suffuses all the histories—from official government histories, to international scholarly histories, to popular histories and biographies on the Internet. The way the story is told, Madame Mao makes a really good villain. She is beautiful, powerful, at once glamorous and stained by the tawdry circumstances of her birth, sexually manipulative and promiscuous, vengeful, merciless, unstable, and unrepentant.

As far back as the days of Qin Shi Huangdi, there was a tradition of unofficial court histories called *yeshi*, in addition to the sanctioned histories of the dynastic court. *Yeshi* can be translated as "also" or "wild" histories. They incorporate the official accounts but also combine rumor and gossip to bend and reconfigure stories into tales that are more entertaining (and sometimes more accurate in spirit) than the official recordings of events.

These also/wild histories were counter-tales to the emperor's powerful versions of the way things went down, not only the big conquering-and-acquiring sorts of things but also the everyday doings among the elite. The *yeshi* disrupted these dominant narratives, coming from below, from the shadows, often detailing the point of view of women and servants. Even in their obvious exaggerations and speculations, they were understood as corrective tales to something the sanctioned accounts might have gotten wrong, or they were different stories, ones that the authors and their constituents would rather be the truth.

These also/wild narratives can be found in many different cultures, surrounding their official histories and canonized texts. The Hebrew Bible includes many of these also/wild versions of events within the Scriptures themselves. The rabbis write fanciful re-imaginings of events, often reassigning the subject of a psalm or a prophetic word. The text becomes about *who* is telling the story and *what is motivating them* to tell it. I love this play of stories and history and meaning and words and ideas. But calling attention to the *yeshi* or the midrash is really like pointing out that the trees in the South American Rainforest are the planet's lungs, producing oxygen for the world to breathe, when of course all the flowers and the weeds in every backyard and boulevard pushing through the cracks in the concrete are working just as hard to turn sunlight into glucose and oxygen.

It's in the nature of a story to point to the teller. So whether you read ancient scriptures or histories or contemporary news reports, it's always a good idea to at least give the teller a quick once-over or a raise of the eyebrow. But it's also in the nature of a good story to draw you into a place where you forget there's a storyteller altogether, which is a great place to be.

Ideally I prefer this unconscious dialectical tension to be present always. "Both/and" is one of my favorite ways to consume and construct a story. Countless other authors play the same way. Playwright Bertolt Brecht was famous for hanging a light too low, below the top of the proscenium, so it was visible, or leaving a stepladder onstage to remind the audience that, even as the acting and plot drew them in emotionally, they were watching a play, so they should remain a bit critical.

Moses did this all the time in Genesis, placing two different versions of a story one right after the other, starting with the creation stories. Some authors want to disappear completely and forever, guiding your every step through the story without your realizing their agenda. Many are historians and writers of sacred texts—or politicians and advertisers. So, when something in a text—a crack or a wrinkle in the rug—catches my foot and trips me up, I've learned, instead of regaining my balance immediately and looking around to see if anyone saw me stumble, to stop. I stop. Or let myself hit the ground and turn around and examine what exactly hiccupped in the narrative. It's not always as pronounced as a stumble—maybe it's just a little something that didn't sit quite right, a note that's a little pitchy. Maybe I feel a growing discomfort; maybe a narrative is driving so hard in one direction that it seems rude or uncool to slow it down and ask some questions.

The absolutely perfect villain I was finding everywhere in Chinese history started to give me pause. Madame Mao and her Gang of Four might have implemented the policies of the Cultural Revolution, but Mao had given them their power, and it was Mao who wrote the declaration of the revolution passed by the Politburo in 1966. He might have been in his bedroom with the curtains drawn, but he was sending regular missives to his wife, pushing the craziness of Maoist worship even further.

In fact, Mao's megalomania brought the country to the brink of collapse twice in its first two decades. But in China today, he is held in great esteem—like George Washington, Thomas Jefferson, Abraham Lincoln, Teddy Roosevelt, and *Moses* put together. There's only one face in Tiananmen Square: the portrait of Mao. It hangs over the Tiananmen

Gate on the north end of the square and is, to the outside world, one of the most iconic images of China. Mao's face—thirty feet tall and twenty-two feet wide—overlooks both the enormous square, designed to hold nearly three quarters of a million people, and the Great Hall of the People, China's house of parliament.

In the center of the square, Mao's preserved body is on display in an elaborate mausoleum. Every morning, thousands of Chinese line up to pay tribute to the Chairman, many bringing flowers.

Madame Mao, on the other hand, is remembered as a monster and serves as the symbol of the violence and excess of the Cultural Revolution. What accounts for this about-face? When Mao died in 1976, Deng Xiaoping and his comrades moved quickly to arrest the Gang of Four. They were stripped of their power and positions, charged with anti-party crimes as well as crimes against the people. A massive media campaign began to discredit them and separate their actions from those of Mao.

It was this campaign, in fact, that created the moniker "Gang of Four," painting the group as crazed political thugs who were stopped just before they attempted to overthrow the government. At the trial, which was televised, Madame Mao was the only one who mounted a defense. She dismissed her attorneys and represented herself, insisting that she was only obeying Mao's orders and acted always to defend his philosophy. "I was Chairman Mao's dog," she famously said. "Whom he said bite, I bit."[5]

---

5. Graham Hutchings, *Modern China* (Cambridge, MA: Harvard University Press, 2001), p. 237.

All four of the Gang were convicted and at first sentenced to death; later the sentence was reduced to life in prison. Eventually, the other three perpetrators were released, but Madame Mao was not, largely because the official media made much of the claim that she refused to repent. In 1991 she was transferred from prison to the hospital to be treated for throat cancer. She committed suicide there, hanging herself in the closet of her hospital room. Reports say that she left this suicide note: "Today the revolution has been stolen by the revisionist clique of Deng Xiaoping. Chairman Mao exterminated Liu Shaoqi, but not Deng, and the result of this omission is that unending evils have been unleashed on the Chinese people and nation. Chairman, your student and fighter is coming to see you!"[6]

In reporting her death, Shanghai's *Liberation Army Daily* newspaper wrote, "The witch has committed suicide."[7]

Perhaps Madame Mao was her husband's shadow side, and the stories of her brutality and unrepentant evil were necessary to keep any stain from the image of the founder of the revolution. While Mao's political philosophy and policies were replaced with Deng's almost immediately after Mao's death, Mao's narrative as the Great Leader and Teacher, the Chairman, was actively promoted.

Ever pragmatic, Deng realized how useful it would be if the people saw Mao and China as inseparable. He could continue to tell the heroic story of Mao while moving the country in the opposite direction without the majority real-

6. Ross Terrill, *Madame Mao: The White-Boned Demon*, rev. ed. (Stanford, CA: Stanford University Press, 1999), p. 353.

7. Reuters, "Official Chinese Commentary Gloats over Death of Mao's Widow," *Los Angeles Times*, June 10, 1991, Memorials sec.

izing it. Indeed, no individual is more responsible for making China what it is today than Deng Xiaoping, but there is no public memorial to him in Tiananmen Square or anywhere in the capital. In 2000, however, a thirty-foot-tall bronze statue of Deng, striding forward, was completed on the Grand Plaza in the center of the Special Economic Zone of Shenzhen.

A CITY IS BORN, a twenty-one-minute film made by the M. Penn Phillips Corporation, was created in 1960 to promote real estate opportunities in Salton City.[8] The film begins with a swell of romantic music, the kind made popular in that era by the likes of the Mitch Miller Orchestra and Lawrence Welk. It's clearly meant to be appealing, maybe even relaxing or beautiful, but I can't help hearing an underlying tension in it, like if I listened close enough, I could pick up the barely audible screams of someone locked in the basement. The screen flashes, showing a valley dotted with homes, and the narrator comes in, sounding like the dad from *Father Knows Best* or *Leave It to Beaver*. Those fifties T.V. dads always sounded like they were trying to teach you something they thought might be hard for you to understand, and they didn't want to cause alarm or convey nonchalance. But they wanted to let you know that this was serious, and while it might be difficult to grasp, you should pay attention and try to understand it.

"The American West," the narrator begins. "You would think there would be enough land to go around. . . ."[9] Real es-

---

8. *Past Pleasures at the Salton Sea: A Collection of Films, Photos, & Music from the Glory Days of the Salton Sea.* Tilapia Film, 2008.
9. *Past Pleasures at the Salton Sea.*

tate growth brings about ever-rising property values, *Father Knows Best* teaches you. But the land becomes overcrowded, and people begin to spread out—to Balboa, to Venice. Now the images change to scenes of beautiful beach towns. And finally, the people push out into the desert, the narrator says, to Palm Springs. Now the film shows images of the desert, then smiling people playing golf and laughing people poolside, then cuts to a shot of the desert, then pans to women and children in swimsuits playing on the beach of a great sea while a speedboat crosses the screen, pulling a waving water skier. "You are witnessing the greatest of man's miracles: bringing life into barrenness."[10]

Now the narrator transitions to a slightly faster pace, his voice more urgent but somehow more welcoming and intimate too. It's like he's thrown his arm around you, pulled you in close, and is speaking in a low voice directly into your ear. He has something just for you, not for all those other jamokes—just you. He explains that the All-American Canal brings fresh water from the Colorado River, so the desert paradise will have all the water it needs for development. This place has it all: the scenic vistas, the mountains, and "another touch of nature's majestic beauty—the Salton Sea."

After the first seven minutes, *A City Is Born* switches from images conjuring up the New Recreation Capital of the World to shots of construction workers and building sites for the rest of the film. There are only a few cuts back to the bikini-clad women, the palm trees, and the swimming pools. But there are lots of long shots of the construction

---

10. *Past Pleasures at the Salton Sea.*

machinery at work. I guess that's the primary power in the war to force the earth to obey man's will. Laying pipe (only the finest asbestos pipe is used, the narrator explains), raising electrical poles, and paving roads with asphalt—the film goes into surprising detail about the building methods.

Salton City even has its own asphalt plant, the narrator explains, then pauses, letting the viewer focus on the glorious asphalt-plant shots: asphalt pouring from chute to chute, trucks being loaded with asphalt, loaded asphalt trucks heading out of the plant.

Where it gets really good, A City Is Born cuts to trucks dumping piles of asphalt on unpaved roads and heavy power equipment smoothing it out. Then the narrator finally says what every viewer is thinking: "Here's the way to really appreciate quality and smoothness. Take a drive on the newly paved asphalt roads." Now the film cuts to the inside of a car, catching the front of the hood, but the star is the asphalt road. The car follows the road around corners and along straightaways, surrounded by nothing but endless biscuit-colored earth obeying man's will, accepting his dominion.

As the screen fades to black, up comes a billboard stuck in the empty desert proclaiming "Now under Construction: Salton Bay Marina and Yacht Club." The screen then shows excavators digging out the final buckets of earth from a wide canal, that earth being the only thing keeping the Salton Sea from flooding into it. The narrator's voice swells to accompany the image: "Here where the mountains, sea, and desert combine to form a magic wonderland is the first man-made marina on the Salton Sea." And the capping line comes next: "Everything has been put into this project for the pleasure of the property owners: planning, imagination, machinery, and money."[11]

As the buckets dig and the sea floods in, finding the low spots in the excavated earth, the narrator says triumphantly, "This is the miracle of man coming to life before your eyes. This is the great marina, designed and constructed to give joy to thousands, built by man for the enjoyment of man. This is the future, today."[12] The music swells again as we witness the water filling up the marina in a crazy re-contextualizing of the breach that caused the Colorado River to flood the desert and create the Salton Sea.

All those people who would be interested in the glamorous life of yacht clubs, nightclubs, marinas, and luxury on the New Riviera—how do you sell them on the dream by making them sit through images of asphalt-making, excavating and paving roads, and digging out a marina? Is heavy machinery really as sexy as Marilyn Monroe?

At that moment it dawned on me: the reason why my working-class grandpa, an Okie whose ideas about money were hard-shaped by the Depression, would buy a piece of vacation property in the Jewel of the California Riviera.

I finally got it: these ambitious developers with their slick films weren't trying to sell lots to the jet-setting, Palm Springs playboys. They were trying to sell the chance to get in first to the hard-working folks who saved every leftover scrap of pipe and length of rope—something that could help them get by, take care of their families, and maybe put away a little for the future. My mom had been right about my grandpa's dream.

---

11. *Past Pleasures at the Salton Sea.*
12. *Past Pleasures at the Salton Sea.*

My grandpa would never sit through a glitzy trailer that was all about swimming pools, yacht clubs, and cocktail parties. But I can see him watching a film about a new development offering an investment opportunity so solid, so legitimate, that it even had its own asphalt plant. He would want to see the heavy equipment, how the ditches were dug and the pipe was laid. He would feel good about investing in a place well-built by hard-working men. The thing that would have sealed the deal was the pitch that he could have something that rich city folks wanted, and they'd have to buy it from him. After a lifetime of always being under, it would be like finally getting over—having a chance to be in control of his own future.

The Salton Sea sellers seemed to invest as much money in promotion, advertising, and sales as they did in the land they were developing. They advertised heavily in the Los Angeles and San Diego areas, running regular buses to the Salton Sea for free vacation weekends. A film they made several years later, in 1968, *A Miracle in the Desert*, featured some of the exact shots of *A City Is Born*, as well as some of the same promises, and some nearly identical narration. But I still felt like I had heard it all somewhere else. Those sales films sounded a lot like the script of Mildred de Stanley's book about the Salton Sea—which, I discovered, seems so odd because it was in fact commissioned as a sales piece. Could there have been a darker intention from the start? To sell as many lots and investment opportunities as possible and never build the houses, the cities, the glorious amenities?

In his first year, M. Penn Phillips sold over 7,000 Salton City lots. Three years later he sold his company to Holly

Sugar, having lost his California business license due to fraudulent business practices. Later that year, the California Department of Fish and Game issued a report saying it believed the Salton Sea would be dead sometime between 1980 and 1990 due to the pollution from agricultural runoff and the rise in salinity. A class-action suit was filed against him, claiming that he knew the future fate of the sea well before the department issued its report, and that he willfully misled investors about the future value of their investments. Phillips responded by moving to Oregon.

Maybe this explains why my grandpa apparently never cashed in on his investment. Did he realize something didn't seem right? Did he try to get his money back? Or was his lot in the Jewel of the California Riviera worthless? Maybe he got swindled.

Maybe the great promise of the shining city was broken. My grandpa thought he was building something for himself, for his family. Instead, he was being sold a bill of goods—a dream with no foundation.

LIKE THE MOLLIES, tilapia were also introduced accidentally into the Salton Sea. In 1975, tilapia were stocked in the All-American Canal to eat up the aquatic plants that clogged the canal system and its drains. Tilapia are a highly invasive species, but they're freshwater fish, so the Irrigation District was confident that even if a few did find their way into the Salton Sea, they wouldn't be able to survive in water that was saltier than the ocean. But it turned out that tilapia are able to adapt to extremely salty water—to thrive in it. Not surprisingly, they quickly found their way into the Salton Sea and made it their own like no species before. So, despite the original plan, no tilapia remained in the canals to eat drain-clogging aquatic plants.

Tilapia is also known as Saint Peter's fish, the name coming from a story in the seventeenth chapter of the Gospel of Matthew. In order to pay the temple tax, Jesus tells Peter to go to the sea and cast a hook, take the first fish that bites, and open its mouth. Inside he will find a coin. Peter does as Jesus says, and pulls a four-drachma coin from the fish's mouth—the exact amount needed to pay the tax. Maybe if the California Department of Fish and Game had been more familiar with the Gospel of Matthew, they could have avoided their half-century-long comedy of errors as they struggled to create a profitable fishing destination at the Salton Sea. Now, eighty-seven years after they began their project and over forty years after the tilapia were accidentally introduced into the sea, everyone seems to know what Peter found out—there's money in tilapia.

Today, tilapia farming is being sold the way raising alpacas once was. Anyone can do it. All you need to do to get started is buy an alpaca from the guy telling you about this amazing opportunity, a little space to breed and raise alpacas, and it's virtually impossible not to make money. Aquaponics & Earth sells a webinar called How to Farm Tilapia for Food, Fun, Fertilizer, & Profit (I'm not kidding) for $198.00, in which the buyer receives $824.00 worth of training (that's $626.00 of free training).[13] On the Aquaculture Tanks website, an informative video on urban aquaculture offers a price breakdown, showing all costs and prof-

---

13. "How to Farm Tilapia for Food, Fun, Fertilizer, & Profit." Aquaponics andearth.org. September 5, 2013. Accessed January 14, 2015.

its using their twelve-tank system: the short story is that an annual investment of $200,270.00 will reap a profit of $407,230.00.[14]

At the other end of the spectrum, tilapia are being sold like corn syrup. Tilapia have been dubbed the aquatic chicken, either because their mild, white meat is reminiscent of the mild, versatile flavor of chicken, or because they can be raised cheaply by the mega-millions on industrial farms.

Today the aquatic chicken is a 1.8 billion-dollar-a-year business, on a par with the trout and salmon industries, and the big tilapia money is in China. According to an article in the *Bloomberg Businessweek* magazine, Chinese tilapia is the future of fish.[15]

The Chinese don't seem to have a taste for it, but Americans can't get enough of it. Eighty percent of the tilapia consumed in the United States is imported from China. Walmart imports 8.8 million pounds—that's 200 shipping containers of frozen Chinese tilapia—a month. Most of it is raised in Guangdong Province, the center of China's manufacturing industries, where behemoth factories manufacture consumer electronics for Apple, Sony, and Toshiba, and every other kind of device, toy, and kitchen appliance. The poor Chinese laborers work like they once did on the Wall, with few other options. Once again, they're building the things that unify their country—and that connect us all, if only technologically.

Guangdong Province is also the center of China's auto industry and most of China's multinational petrochemical

14. "Tilapia," Aquaculture Tanks. Accessed January 14, 2015.

15. Bruce Einhorn, "From China, The Future of Fish," *Bloomberg Businessweek* magazine, October 21, 2010. Accessed January 14, 2015.

plants. The working conditions and pollution levels are regularly criticized as unacceptable by international human rights and environmental organizations. Even the pro-Beijing newspaper *South China Morning Post* regularly reports on the dangerous air and water quality. Acid rain and industrial runoff contaminate the soil and the water.[16]

The large factory farms devoted to tilapia require enormous amounts of fresh water to continually flush out the tilapia feces and other materials from the growing ponds that can affect the taste of the fish. The tilapia farmer interviewed in the *Bloomberg Businessweek* article said that the amount of water wasn't a problem. Under a special program to promote aquaculture, the government had built canals to bring water to all the farmers for free.

There are more than 250 factories in the area that process the fish. It is butchered, skinned, frozen, and covered in a carbon-monoxide glaze that keeps the fish looking fresh beyond the point where it would begin to break down.

As it turns out, tilapia are on the International Union for Conservation of Nature's list of 100 of the World's Worst Invasive Alien Species.[17] Apparently they so dominated the resources in the Salton Sea that the mollies and the corvina, once the heart of the sea's fishery, couldn't hold their own. And today, tilapia are the only fish found in the Salton Sea.

---

16. "Beijing Air Pollution," *South China Morning Post* Topics. http://www.scmp.com/topics/beijing-air-pollution. Accessed January 14, 2015.

17. Sarah J. Lowe, *100 of the World's Worst Invasive Alien Species: A Selection from the Global Invasive Species Database*. Updated and reprinted version, 2004.

CHAPTER 9

Lamenting the Internet . . .
Finding Ourselves at the Salton Sea . . .
Inching toward the Great Wall . . .
"Don't Think about the Way Down" . . .
First Aggression, then Deterioration . . .
Let's Call Them Ripple Effects . . .

To lament. The English word not only expresses regret about a situation or a loss; it suggests regret *and* grief—deep sorrow, expressed physically and audibly, like wailing.

The Hebrew origin of the word *lament* means "how." Like: How the hell did we wind up like this, how could this be happening? And, pretty pointedly, how could God have done this to us? The book of Lamentations in the Old Testament is called that because the first word in the book is "How."

The tone is bleak: God does not speak, the degree of suffering is presented as undeserved, and expectations of future redemption are minimal. Things are bad, end-of-days bad, dystopian-future bad, post-nuclear-launch bad. And it is God's fault.

The book of Lamentations was written during the Exile, the Babylonian Exile. This was the time when the conquering Babylonian army carried away a bunch of Judahites to make them slaves in Babylon—but more than that, the Babylonian army desecrated the temple, the house where God lived, desecrated the Holy of Holies, and then completely destroyed the temple and razed to the ground the city of God: Jerusalem.

With their country a wasteland of rubble and blood, poisoned wells and salted fields—a place where life was no longer possible—the people of God were brought to Babylon. They blamed God, and why wouldn't they? God's house, God's city, God's promised land had been brought to ruin. So where was God?

Reading Lamentations from my own historical and theological context, it is clear to me that it is not God who is torturing God's own people. It is the dominant and dominating power of the region—the Babylonian Empire. But it is hard for God's people to conceive that the empire could be stronger than God, so they think God must be using the empire in some way to punish them, that God must be cooperating with the empire. The two are somehow conflated. Or God is just gone. The distance between God and the people has grown so great that God doesn't notice them being taken away.

Has another empire taken us away? Are we wondering how God lost sight of us? Or how we lost sight of God? Everywhere I hear sighs of lament. Including my own.

Lament at the Dawn of the Internet Empire
How did we let you come and take away our souls?
You promised more food, cheaper food,
>   but you fed us poison, and raped our once-fertile
>   fields.
You disfigured our bodies from the inside out. Our guts
>   belong to you.

Our blood and the blood of our children runs cold,
  full of your chemicals and heavy metals.
Our lungs fill with particulates from abandoned
  products made to improve our lives until
  the body count got too high.
You have pulled our sons and daughters, mothers and
    fathers
  into endless war—over energy or territory or pride or
  projection of power.
Or perhaps for reasons so nefarious
  that we will never know them.
But our soldiers come back, brain-injured, disfigured,
  hopeless, legless, no prospects.
While your air force, barely children, sit in Arizona
  with their joysticks and screens,
killing other people's children, brothers, mothers
  across the globe, the death droning on and on.
You have stolen our minds with promises of knowledge
    and choice and power,
promises of fame and joy and love.
And we have been possessed, or accessed,
  numbed or persuaded by the mundane
  disguised as the magnificent.
All that we have left we give you freely, willingly—
  our privacy, our desires, our needs, our friends
    and neighbors.
Now you can process everyone, everything, every
    feeling,
and tell us who we are, what we want, and what we
    think.
You have stolen our souls, and we have not noticed,

would actually prefer not to notice,
so that we may live on and on forever,
in a place where our profiles will never be deleted.
Humming eternally on inside servers
lost in the middle of a great desert.

MY BROTHER AND I left the restaurant where we'd met Al Kalin and loaded the faithful Prius for our circumnavigation of the Salton Sea. Sunglasses and water were our main concerns. I was grateful to be setting off on this last part of our research trip/spiritual quest with the tensions Al had provided. He loved farming, and he loved the Salton Sea. Each contained the seed that created the other, and each held the elements that would lead to the destruction of the other.

The seeds of mutual creation and destruction . . . The phrase kept coming back to me as Mike and I made one more stop before we set out on our final journey.

When I moved to Brawley the first time, I went to work with my dad as the youth director at the First Baptist Church of Brawley. I was in a weird place, having been informed by the business office at my college that I wouldn't be allowed to register for the second semester until I paid my bill for the first semester. Hard to do, since I didn't have any money.

As foreign as Imperial Valley and Brawley were to me, there was something about that foreignness that freed me to be a little less self-conscious, to worry a little less about who I should be or how I should be—it was the freaking desert, after all. Nobody had many options. We were here, we were who we were, and we had to live together. Live and let live.

Okay, it was a little like that, but not completely. The

place was basically run by hardcore men, farmers and ranchers who worked hard and generally didn't share their feelings. I think the hardcore men thought I was a weirdo or an idiot—which I was in their world. Once I was out checking fields with the father of a girl in my youth group. I wanted to try to relate to him because I cared about this girl, and in my one semester of college I had read about Family Systems Theory. I think the dad took me out to check the fields with him because he loved his daughter, and if it was important to her, he would try to get to know me.

I remember standing on a melon field that had been harvested, and he had contracted to put cattle on it—the cattle would feed on the produce the harvesters had missed. We were waiting for the cattle transport trucks, and he bent down and picked up a melon, a cantaloupe, brushed the dirt off it, and handed it to me. "Here," he said. "Taste that. It's sweet, it's good." I took it, fully aware of the meaning of the gesture. He was trying to connect. I held the cantaloupe in my hands, looked at it, smelled it, and then, after an awkward pause, he said again, "Go on, taste it." I didn't know what to do, having only eaten cantaloupe cut in half in a bowl or cut up in a fruit salad.

"Go on," he repeated.

"Um, how do I eat it?" I asked apologetically.

Exasperated, he said, "Just cut it open with your knife and then cut yourself off a piece."

I was awash in embarrassment. "Um, I don't have a knife."

He looked at me, not angry but baffled. It was pre-judgment, like he was honestly trying to comprehend. "You don't have a knife?"

I shook my head.

Then, in judgment or exasperation, he grabbed the melon from my hands. From his back pocket he took out his folding knife, snapped it open, and in three elegant moves cut the cantaloupe in half, sliced a half into squares, and speared one of the squares on the knifepoint and presented it to me. Later that day I bought a folding knife. At all the youth-group fundraisers and performances after that, he was always there front-and-center for his daughter, but he never said another word to me, and honestly, I was glad.

You don't have a knife? Yeah, now I have a knife. I'm a normal person—of course I have a knife.

The thing was, I didn't spend a lot of time with the farmers and ranchers. At the church I spent time with their elderly parents, with their wives and their kids—and they loved me. The kids and the wives didn't want to be stuck in Imperial Valley, they wanted more, and I was from the city and expressed more than two emotions. I knew about music and movies and books, and I had been to New York City. The old-timers had mellowed from their hardcore Men of Renown days and liked my interest in their lives and their stories. They were old enough to allow themselves to be curious and not resistant to someone different from them.

Honestly, it wasn't completely the foreignness of Imperial Valley that gave me a kind of freedom in its otherness. It was that I thought I was better than the people around me. I knew more things and had had more experiences. And I was smarter. Before, I had always felt out of place, but also like I wasn't enough. I wasn't smart enough, I was poor, I was different. I was looked down on or was the less fortunate one they tried to help. But in Brawley, with the wives and the kids and the old-timers, I was the guy from *somewhere else*—from college, from the city, from back East. It felt good to be one of the people who felt good. I confessed this to Mike. "Is it really bad that I felt this way?"

"I felt the exact same way," he told me. "We were poor and Baptist and weird. But when I was in Brawley, I never felt like a loser. There were just so many people there who were way more poor, way more Baptist, and way more weird."

The First Baptist Church of Brawley was on the edge of town, on the corner of Highway 86 and Legion Road. And I belonged there. When I left to go back to college, the church had a ceremony for me, a kind of roast and a potluck. It was a place that meant something to me.

Two years later, while finishing college in Seattle, I read Douglas Coupland's *Generation X: Tales for an Accelerated Culture*. It defined my generation, literally named my generation, gave us a chance to crawl out from under the oppressive cultural collapse of the baby boomers. But even more, this novel named me, got me, snagged me as I was floating off into space and brought me back, concluding with a chapter titled "Jan. 01, 2000" [a decade after the publication of the book]: *On the corner of Highway 86 and Legion Road.*

This corner was right across the street from the First Baptist Church of Brawley. I was in disbelief as I read the first paragraph: "I drove to Calexico this afternoon by way of the Salton Sea, a huge saline lake and the lowest elevation in the U.S. I drove through the Box Canyon, through El Centro . . . Calipatria . . . Brawley. . . . I entered the region in a good mood at the lemon groves of a small citrus town called Mecca. I'd just stolen a warm orange the size of a bowling ball from a roadside grove and a farmer rounding a corner on a tractor had caught me; all he did was smile, reach into a bag beside him, and throw me another. A farmer's forgiveness felt very absolute."[1]

The protagonist continued on Highway 86 and saw in the distance a huge roiling cloud, a mushroom cloud. If you grew up in the 1980s with Ronald Reagan broadcasting the talking points he was given, you considered it a very real possibility that the world would end this way.

The protagonist drove on, toward the mushroom cloud, convinced it was the end of the world, until, "at last, at the Highway 86 junction where I turned sharply right, I was able to see the root of this mushroom. Its simple source both made instant sense and filled me with profound relief: farmers within a small area were burning off the stubble of their fields. The stratospheric black monster created by the frail orange ropes of flame that ran across their fields was insanely out of proportion to the deed—this smoke cloud visible for five hundred miles—*visible from outer space*."[2]

These are Doug Coupland's italics, not mine.

This place, this exact junction meant something to me, to the narrative—to the universes. So before Mike and I circumnavigated the Salton Sea, we paid a little homage to the location. We decided to read aloud the passage in the closing chapter of *Generation X* on the very spot where we had lived out important experiences in our lives and where, for some cosmic reason, Douglas Coupland had chosen to end his seminal novel.

At the intersection of Highway 86 and Legion Road,

---

1. Douglas Coupland, "Jan. 01, 2000," in *Generation X: Tales for an Accelerated Culture* (New York: St. Martin's Press, 1991), p. 175.

2. Coupland, *Generation X*, p. 176.

crossways from the First Baptist Church of Brawley, on the very field Coupland describes, there was a new commercial development anchored by a Wal-Mart and including a restaurant, a convenience store, and a carwash. It carried a kind of ambient significance.

I parked the Prius in the church lot, and Mike and I walked to the corner of the lot facing the former field, now carwash et al., and took in the scene. I held up the book and read from it. Mike took a picture of me with the book. We looked around again, and then Mike looked at me. "Is this one of those things that seems like it would be meaningful when you talk about it, but actually doing it feels kind of dumb?"

"Yes," I said. We both laughed. "Let's go. Let's go circumnavigate the Salton Sea." I thrust *Generation X* forward like a bayonet in a charge gesture.

"Woo-hoo!" We bounded back to the Prius. Somehow the acknowledgment of the contrived significance we attempted made us giddy. We got in the car, shaking our heads bemusedly. "We're lame," Mike said.

"*So* lame," I agreed. Then I yelled another "Woo-hoo!" and thrust my fist out the window as I pulled out of the parking lot into the intersection of Highway 86 and Legion Road.

"And super lame," Mike said, pointing at the Wal-Mart. "These places all look brand-new—the Wal-Mart, the Circle K—like if we would have come a week ago, it would still be a field, still be Douglas Coupland's burning field. It's kind of perfect."

"KIND OF PERFECT?" I yelled, still in my giddy *charge* mode, pointing to the sign on the carwash.

"Perfect," Mike read. "Perfect Carwash."

"We have no choice," I said. "We're getting this car washed perfectly." I pulled into the empty lane, put my credit card in the terminal slot and selected the "Ultimate Perfect Wash," maneuvered onto the conveyor belt, and put the Prius in neutral. The belt started moving us forward. Water sprayed and foam exuded from somewhere, covering the windows, and robot arms circled the car as we rolled along. "Pret-ty perfect," Mike nodded—right before we heard a loud thwack from the back of the car.

We both turned around: the rear windshield wiper was gone, along with the whole oscillating arm, the mechanism broken off at the base. All the woo drained from my hoo. Before I could even check out the damage, I had to wait for the conveyor belt to slowly convey the car to the end of the wash. The robot arms continued to circle around, unconcerned with the violence they had just committed. I pulled out into the parking lot, jumped out of the car, and went around the back to inspect. "What the hell?" I said to Mike, to the universe, to the notion of *perfect*. I could feel myself getting really angry. "I mean, come on. I just, spur of the moment, pull into this carwash, just because—just for the fun of it. It didn't even occur to me if the car needed to be washed. I just pulled in and picked the 'Ultimate Perfect Wash'—not because I was concerned with the level of clean I wanted—I just thought it sounded funny—*and then*—bam!" I hit the top of the car for emphasis as I said "bam" again. "Can you believe this?" I asked Mike, or the universe. "They have to pay for this, right? It's a new carwash. They can't let their robot arms go ripping things off cars. I'm going to tell them, show them, make them pay."

Mike was looking at me like he knew he should have my back, but also like he thought I should bring it down several notches. "Yeah, that's a drag."

"A drag? I'm going to talk to someone right now." I went into the office, looked the high school girl sitting at the desk straight in the eyes, and demanded to see the owner. He wasn't there, she said. Then I demanded to see the manager. There wasn't a manager, she said. I challenged that and explained what had happened. She seemed as unconcerned as the robot arms. Then Mike walked in. He had found the remains of my wiper arm in the carwash bay. "Look," I said to her emphatically, pointing at the pieces in Mike's hands. She looked at them and then looked at her phone, reading a text. I asked her what she was going to do about it. She said she didn't know.

"I think we could fix it pretty easily. I don't think the parts would cost that much," Mike said in a deliberately calm voice, taking a step back, trying to coax me to the door. Just then a man came out of the back room wearing an overly bright uniform shirt and walked straight into my personal space.

"I'm sorry," he said. "There's nothing we can do."

"Are you the manager?" I asked. He said there was no manager. When I asked if he was the owner, he said no. At that point I demanded he give me the owner's number. He told me that the sign at the carwash entrance explains that they are not responsible for certain kinds of damage.

"A windshield wiper being ripped off by your robot arms? Does the sign say that?" I demanded.

"Yes," he said.

"Well, I want the owner's number. You broke my car and you're going to fix it." He clearly didn't like the way I was talking to him. He grabbed a Post-it note and scribbled down a number.

"Now, if you will please leave," he said, handing me the yellow square of paper.

"I'm not going to leave until someone tells me what they're going to do about my car." When I said that, he took half a step forward, and I saw beyond the overly bright shirt—I saw the rest of him. He was at least four inches taller than I was, and since his chest was at my eye level, I could easily see that he worked out.

"Let's go," Mike said.

"What is the name?" I demanded, tilting my head back to look him in the eye. "What is the owner's name?" He grabbed the Post-it, wrote a name in block letters, and pushed the paper back in my hand.

"Now, we'd like to get back to our business," he said, making a dismissive gesture with his hand.

"Not before I call the owner." I pulled out my phone and stabbed the number in with righteous anger. I held it to my ear and gave him a nod, like *Now we'll see who's responsible*. It rang and rang. No answer. I dialed the number again. It rang and rang. I held the phone out to the man so he could hear it ringing. "No answer," I said, like I had caught him in a lie. He didn't look at the phone. He was looking at me, and he seemed very angry. "The sign clearly says we are not liable for certain types of damage, including damage to windshield wipers."

I can't stand to be ripped off, but I saw right then that he was about to punch me. His eyes had darkened, and there was a little twitch in his right bicep. I stepped back, and Mike opened the door and held it for me.

I backed out yelling, "It was not *perfect!*"

HOW YOU EXPERIENCE the Great Wall of China depends on which part of it you visit. The Juyongguan section of the Great Wall is closest to Beijing and offers the most user-friendly experience. Here, the wide stone wall, with its impressive towers and famous "cloud platform," is so pristine that it's hard to believe it's more than five hundred years old. Perhaps that's because it isn't. While the origins of this section of the Wall might be that ancient, the Juyongguan Gate was almost completely rebuilt before the 2008 Beijing Olympics.

Visiting this part of the Wall has other advantages. It features two terra-cotta warriors, so you don't have to make the 700-mile-trip to Shaanxi to see the collection of them that depicts the armies of Qin Shi Huangdi. Nearby is a temple to tour, an espresso bar, plenty of restaurants, and two sky-rides to bring you to the top of the Wall, where you can bungee-jump or take the toboggan slide down.

In 2005, the largest skateboard-related structure in history was erected there so that professional skateboarder and mega-ramp pioneer Danny Way could jump the Great Wall. A tower was built high above the Wall so that Way could drop in with enough height to reach the fifty miles per hour he would need to clear the Wall. On the day of the jump, Way climbed the tower with some skepticism about the quality of the work the Chinese crew had done. His own engineer had continually asked them to build the tower and the ramp according to the plans, but they had waved him off and continued building it their way. When Way reached the top of the tower, which nearly reached heaven, and stood with his skateboard on the edge, preparing to drop into the nearly vertical mega-ramp, he noticed that the tower was swaying six inches from side to side. Even so, he went for it, hitting the perfect speed and clearing the Wall easily—twice. But the day before, during a practice run, he had severely sprained his ankle and cut a huge gash in his arm. The Wall and the tower could just as easily have killed him.

I hired a car to take my family to the Simatai section of the Great Wall, seventy-five miles outside of Beijing. The goal was to be far away from the city, where we would find fewer people, fewer tourists, less rebuilding of the Wall—and more breathable air. During the long ride there, we all slumped against each other, already run down before we even started, our bodies not resisting the bouncing and jouncing from the car's worn-out struts. When we pulled into the visitors' parking lot in Simatai, we turned to face the Wall. But all we saw was a row of hawkers' booths.

"*Lai, lai. Lai, lai,*" multiple voices beckoned or demanded: "Come here. Come here." I looked above and beyond them and saw the side of a mountain rising. I knew that the Wall ran along the ridge of the mountains here, but for some reason I had never imagined that we would have to climb the mountain to get to it. I shielded my eyes from the sun and searched the ridge: I saw nothing but biscuit-colored earth and scrub trees. How could anyone imagine that the Great Wall of China was visible from outer space? I couldn't make it out from the parking lot.

"*Lai, lai. Lai, lai. Ni mai shui? Ni mai shui?*": "Come here. Come here. Do you need water?" I had inadvertently made eye contact with one of the hawkers as I tried to estimate the distance of our climb. After I bought six waters, two Great Wall of China baseball caps, and a battery-operated personal fan, we were on our way. I had very little resistance left in me. It seemed easier to give them money than to try to explain why I didn't want to. It seemed the quickest way to get free. Still, we walked toward the base of the mountain to a chorus of "*Wei lai. Wei lai. Wei lai.*" ("Come back. Come back. Come back.") Fewer tourists mean they have to work the ones they get that much harder.

We started out on the designated mountain path. After twenty minutes of walking, the path split into two parts. One headed into the foothills; the other went fifteen feet up to a chairlift. My family paused at the fork, a couple of steps toward the chairlift, and turned to me with tired, questioning eyes. I think my reputation in the family made them sure that I would insist we climb up the mountain, that a chairlift would be some sort of compromise, an invalidation of the authenticity of the experience.

And normally I would have been that much of an imperious twit, but I was even more spent than they were. I smiled in sort of a gracious, nurturing way, as if I were making a concession out of my love for them. This way I retained the moral high ground, and I got to ride up in a chairlift. It took us three-quarters of the distance, and though we could transfer to another that would take us to the top, Jeanne and I agreed to force our children to climb the rest of the way.

We still had a long trek ahead of us. And the path was a narrow, single-file rut most of the way, with switchback after switchback. I could see the Wall if I tilted my head back to the sky, but doing that made me feel like I was going to tumble off the side of the mountain. I was sure that dozens of people took that tumble every year. This wasn't an OSHA-approved path. It was getting kind of scary, especially every time an elderly German couple overtook us. Joe and I started slowing down, being a bit more deliberate with our footsteps. Jeanne and Maria seemed invigorated by the prospect of reaching the top. "You go ahead." I called to them. "I'll stay back with Joe." Soon they were out of sight.

When Joe and I finally got to the base of the Wall, it was twenty feet of stone straight up. A set of narrow stone stairs ran up the side, with no railing or handholds or caution tape. "Let's just go," I said to Joe. "Go slow and don't look over the side." We both found the same technique for navigating the stairs: we put our right hand on the step, our left hand on the wall for support, and sort of crawled up, step by step. Eventually we reached the top. We pulled ourselves over the edge onto the Wall walk and slowly stood up.

It was breathtaking. It was the Great Wall of China. It's so rare when something can withstand the countless accolades heaped upon it and come out seeming even more spectacular. But the Wall definitely did that. It swept out in front of me, following the contours of the mountain ridge, undulating and meandering, vanishing at the earth's horizon. I looked straight up, just in case someone was looking down from outer space. I smiled and waved.

"Papa," Maria called out from behind us. I turned and saw the Wall, rising steeply up in steps to a high tower. She bounded down the crumbling stairs, the width of the Wall here no more than eight feet, nothing but a short stone lip on either side and then a straight drop off the Wall and down the side of the mountain.

"*Ni mai shui? Ni mai shui?*" Out of nowhere came two old women, pushing bottles of water at Joe and me, trying to talk over each other, competing for my business.

"*Bu hao, bu hao, bu hao!*" I said emphatically, waving my arms in the universal sign for *Get away from me—I'm freaking out*. This I was able to successfully communicate. The women retreated, then disappeared. Now Maria stood next to me on the step, grabbing my arm.

"Let's catch up with Mama."

"*Let go! Let go! Let go!*" I almost shouted, feeling like she could destabilize me and send me tumbling. She breezed past me to catch up with Jeanne. Joe and I looked into each other's eyes, and I'm sure we were thinking the same thing: *We're on top of a narrow, crumbling wall on top of a mountain.* Slowly I began to squat down, and Joe followed my lead. I got down on my knees and eased forward until I was lying flat on top of the Wall. When I turned my head to the right to look at Joe, he lay there next to me. I squeezed my eyes shut. He reached out, took my hand, and said, "Don't think about the way down."

AT BREAKFAST, Al had told Mike and me that there were places where we would find the future of the Salton Sea—and one of those was the state park. When we got there, we turned into the campground and boat launch at the south end of the park, looking for a way to get to the water. The state park is fourteen miles of shoreline from Bombay Beach to the north end of the Salton Sea. According to the California parks website, it's great for fishing, kayaking, and camping, with full RV hook-ups and a visitor center.

All those great things must have been located at the other end of the park. And the road—I couldn't tell if it was unpaved or simply deteriorated. Mike was driving cautiously forward. We had already gotten stuck in the desert dirt up to our axle, and we didn't want to chance it again, given the blistering heat and the pervasive vibe that no one had camped or boat-launched here in a very long time. If we weren't careful, we would end up being just another couple of shriveled dead things for someone to point at and say, "Ewww, gross," in their YouTube video—shot right before Triple A came to save us.

"I think the road ran out," Mike said, stopping the Prius. "Let's walk." It was less than a quarter-mile to the water's edge, but it was so hot and so bright. We moved slowly, breathing with our mouths open. Halfway to the water we came across a cinderblock-and-wood building, graffiti-ed and ruined. The door and the windows on one side were missing, and most of two walls were gone on the other. A twisted clump of rebar stuck out from the concrete foundation like thin, arthritic fingers grasping for the missing walls, unsuccessfully trying to keep them from leaving. At one time this may have been the park's restrooms and showers, but now the wiring and the plumbing were all stripped out. And the desert had come inside, the wind and the salt wearing down any sharp edges on the cinderblock and wood joists. But this building had first met its fate through aggression, not deterioration. These two elements often work hand in hand out here.

Just past the building's carcass and the skeletal remains of a couple dozen tilapia, a road seemed to appear. Well, big cement slabs, broken and tilting, mostly uncovered by the dirt. These continued at a slight decline for about sixty feet and then stopped.

"Evidence of a road," I said to Mike, making the laying-it-all-on-the-table gesture.

"Boat ramp," he countered.

I looked down at the concrete slabs, noticing the small ridging running across their width, and then I looked up and out. The edge of the sea was still 180 feet away. Mike and I walked to the end of the ramp, realizing it was absurd to think of a sparkling boat on a trailer hitched to a shiny, big-man pick-up truck backing up along this stretch. The ravaged building and the broken slabs were marooned in the desert. There was no road to get the magnificent truck and trailered boat to the start of the ramp, and no water at the end of it. Just the hard, dry earth.

Looking toward the sea from the end of the ramp, looking up and down the shoreline, I could see the flat expanse, more gray than the pale desert floor, marked sporadically with bright white pools of salt. A steady wind blew, and I tasted salt and some other acrid thing, felt them on my skin. This was the future of the Salton Sea.

"A lot of people think the accident in 1905 created the Salton Sea, but it didn't. There has always been a sea, off and on, in the Colorado Desert." Al had explained the cycle that morning. If there was a really wet year or the delta got plugged up and the Colorado River flooded, it would fill up the Salton Sink. After the flooding ended, the water would start to dry up. The sea evaporates at a pretty constant rate of six feet a year. So, depending on how big the floods were, that could take a while. In 1890, ten years before work started on the first canal, there was a 200,000-acre lake in the Sink. There was even some water in the Sink when the accident happened.

The Colorado draining into the desert and forming a giant body of water was nothing new. But the enormous blunder that created the body of water known as the Salton Sea was the first time humans ever made it happen. These Men of Renown accidentally triggered the ancient flooding cycle and then interrupted it. With the canals bringing water to the fields and the runoff water flowing into the Salton Sea, it would never dry up. It still evaporated at the rate of six feet a year, but given the annual amount of the excess agricultural water (varied only by hurricanes), the surface has remained a fairly constant 234 feet below sea level.

So there you have it. These Heroes of Old tamed the Colorado River: it was never going to flood the delta again, because the water would be gone before it had a chance to get there. These men had taken what was briefly seen as a catastrophic failure and shown it to be a great gift to both man and woman, to the birds of the air and to the fish in the sea and to all the things that creep upon the earth (especially the developers of the desert paradise). Unlike nature's lakes in the desert, theirs wasn't going to dry up.

Until now.

This trouble has been in the works for a while. The sea kept filling up at about one million acre-feet a year (one acre-foot would supply two families for a year). Until 1995, that is, when the perfect storm started building—and by "perfect storm" I mean a man-made environmental disaster. The effects of global warming were beginning to be evident as California entered its longest drought in recorded history. By 2014, 90 percent of the state was in severe or extreme drought conditions. This means that less water flows into the Salton Sea from natural sources. Meanwhile, the millions of people on the other side of the mountains in San Diego are getting really thirsty. They see all that water running off those fields and into that nasty sea, and drool—or would if they weren't so parched.

The Imperial Irrigation District has the rights to 20 percent of the total water allotment of the Colorado River. It was the California Land Development Company's original sales pitch of "As much free water as you can use!" that drew the farmers and ranchers to risk buying acres in the desert. Today the Imperial Valley farmers use all that increasingly precious water to grow 80 percent of the country's winter vegetables.

"The temperature of the Salton Sea never gets below 50 degrees," Al Kalin explained. "As the wind blows across it from the north, it warms up the air so all the fields south of the sea can grow all that baby spinach you like to have in your stores in the winter."[3] A lot of water is also used to grow Bermuda grass and alfalfa hay, which is sold to Asian countries. Dr. Robert Glennon, a University of Arizona water policy expert, calculated that in 2012, fifty billion gallons of Western water were used in the production of hay that went to China. So while the California water crisis is growing, we are in essence exporting the Colorado River to China.[4]

BACK IN 2003, the state and local water agencies got together in an attempt to balance the needs of the farmers and the urban areas, resulting in what is known as the Quantification Settlement Agreement.

This agreement requires the Imperial Irrigation District to deliver an increasing amount of water to San Diego and

---

3. Personal interview with the author in July 2013.

4. Ben Jervey, "Exporting the Colorado River to Asia, Through Hay," Nationalgeographic.com., January 23, 2014. Accessed January 14, 2015.

the Coachella Valley over the next seventy-five years. Which means less water for agriculture. The difference is supposed to be made up through water-saving programs—for example, the Imperial Irrigation District lines dirt canals with concrete to stop water loss through seepage, and the farmers are supposed to use on-farm conservation technologies. As a result of these water-saving measures, there is less and less water flowing into the Salton Sea. The QSA requires the Imperial Irrigation District to make up for this loss of run-off water by putting a certain amount of water directly into the sea. According to the agreement, this mitigation water, as it's called, will stop being supplied in 2017, which means that the Salton Sea will begin to dry up. At that point the Imperial Irrigation District is required to spend millions of dollars to mitigate the environmental damage caused by the shrinking sea.

Once the required amount of money is spent, which could happen in less than a decade, the state of California is financially responsible for programs designed to lessen the damaging impact of the water shortage on the natural world, including the birds, the fish, and the humans. So the state established an agency to develop a plan to save the Salton Sea after 2017. Several proposals were made, but none of them was funded or acted on by the legislature.

As years went by and this inaction was brought to their attention, they took a look at the price tag on the proposals—starting from nine billion dollars and jumping up sharply from there—and passed legislation granting a few million dollars for a feasibility study instead. It seems that any time their lack of action is pointed out, they fund another study, because the proposed solutions cost so much more than the studies. Based on the state's actions in the years since the Quantification Settlement Agreement, it appears that nothing of any consequence will be done to save the Salton Sea from drying up.

But why not let it dry up? If it was created by accident and there is a historic, natural cycle of flooding and evaporating, why not just let nature take its course? Some folks would argue for that. Other people say that no matter what course of action is taken, the complete evaporation of the Salton Sea is inevitable. Whether inevitable or not, the evaporating Salton Sea brings with it increasingly dire consequences.

Since the Heroes of Old, the Men of Renown altered this ancient symbiotic ecosystem, there have been what you might call ripple effects. There's the evaporation rate, of course. Then there's the increasing salinity of the sea, due to the constant inflow from agricultural runoff (about a ton of salt per acre). And we can't forget the residual toxins from the fertilizer that hitch a ride with the runoff. With all of these elements combined, the Salton Sea will soon reach a point where it can no longer sustain life. Even the heat-loving, salt-loving, seemingly indestructible tilapia won't survive. An unprecedented fish kill could happen almost overnight.

The California Department of Fish and Wildlife believes that salt levels of 60 parts per thousand would be fatal to much of the nearly half a billion tilapia. The Salton Sea's current salt concentration is 52 parts per thousand. And the department admits that the sea could reach the 60-parts-per-thousand threshold in just one year after the Imperial Irrigation District stops supplying the mitigation water in 2017.

And the fallout won't be pretty. The sudden death of hundreds of millions of fish will be a rotting, stinking nightmare of biblical proportions. And the numerous birds who depend on the sea's fishery for food will be left with no place else to go, since 90 percent of California's wetlands have disappeared during the time this accidental body of water enticed hundreds of species to alter their migration patterns.

As the Salton Sea evaporates, it will expose acres and acres of playa—the dried seabed filled with highly concentrated levels of salt and agricultural chemical residue. Dust storms will pick up this toxic mix, which will singe the leaves of the much-desired baby spinach. And if nothing is done, this man-made natural disaster could destroy farming in Imperial Valley, drive countless species of birds to extinction, and have serious effects on the health of scores of people as they regularly breathe in the noxious dust.

Lament at the Dusk of Human Ambition

How has humanity collectively come back
    to the same bleak shore,
Standing in Noah's shadow, staring out at
    the downside of a holy promise?
Now the post-deluge desert is ours, the destruction
    of almost every living thing our grim legacy.
Our desire to make, build, create has seared a dark
    void into the broken heart of the earth.
Once Noah stood on dry land again, a rainbow arcing
    its colors across a clear sky.
Now we stand at the edge of a receding sea,
    its rank waters fetid with the remains of our
        misguided creation.

As we breathe in the stench we call air, surrounded by
    the rubble of our past ambition,
We cannot help but look up,
    filled with persistent longing and voiceless hope.

CHAPTER 10

The Sonny Bono Salton Sea National Wildlife Refuge . . .
Deeper into the Desert . . .
"So You Really Believe in Love, Then?" . . .
The Remains of Bombay Beach . . .
The Ruins of Empire . . .
Finding Myself at an Intersection . . .

Just past the Brawley city limit sign on the west side of Highway 86, an Imperial Irrigation District billboard warns, in staccato sentences and stark, sans-serif letters, *Canals are dangerous. Stay away. Stay alive.* On the east side of the highway, as if to offer an example, the Central Main Canal splits up—one portion spills over a gate and drops twelve feet into the Rookwood Canal, and the rest of the Central Main Canal is sucked down, disappearing underground. It runs, subterranean, along Highway 86, past Legion Road, past Douglas Coupland's former field, past the Circle K and the so-called Perfect Carwash. I don't know where it comes up.

Turning west with the four-lane as it becomes Main Street, I can still feel the anger burn in my arms and the center of my chest. The heat is radiating from me, filling the violated Prius with a stifling intensity.

"What's the big deal?" Mike asks. "It's a windshield wiper."

"No, it's the whole oscillating mechanism thing too. That owner guy ripped me off. And I hate to be ripped off and, like, disregarded."

"He was totally going to punch you."

"I know," I say, thinking it's kind of ridiculous that I pushed it that far, almost funny how ridiculous I am. But then my jaw tightens again, and I shake my head, feeling the burn heat up a notch.

"Just forget it."

"Yeah," I say, without agreeing, looking at the Post-it still in my hand.

The road dips, crossing the New River, and climbs the west bank, leveling out where Brandt turns into Webster Road. I tell Mike to take a right onto Kalin Road, and we follow it to the New River and then wind our way along the banks to as close as we can get to where it empties into the Salton Sea.

The areas around the outlets of the New and Alamo rivers are currently known as the Sonny Bono Salton Sea National Wildlife Refuge. More than four hundred species of birds have been recorded there. It's a key stop-over location on the Pacific Flyway. Ninety-three species make their nests there. It's also the flash-point for the looming man-made natural disaster that is the Salton Sea. The U.S. Fish and Wildlife Service, which manages the refuge, offers this description of it on its website: "The Sonny Bono Salton Sea National Wildlife Refuge was established in 1930 by executive order as a breeding ground for birds and wild animals." Currently the primary objective might include the *management* of endangered, sensitive species and wintering waterfowl, but the refuge was originally established to keep the damn birds off the farmers' fields.

Because these lush green fields, regularly flooded with fresh water, grew where there was once only endless, dry desert, birds on the Pacific Flyway began changing their migratory patterns. But, after all the monumental work that went into irrigating the desert, it would do no good to let it go to the birds. So the Department of the Interior set about creating more desirable habitats for the birds at the south end of the Salton Sea, filling it with trees and plant life particularly attractive to the various species that were showing up. When a thriving fish population was finally established in the 1950s, an astonishing number of birds began frequenting the Salton Sea. In recent years nearly two-thirds of all bird species observed in the United States have been present at the sea.

While these wetland habitats were being created on the Salton Sea, natural wetlands were being drained and destroyed by rapid development in the state. Now, 90 percent of California's wetlands are gone. The birds don't really have any place to go *but* the sea. Unfortunately, the conditions inherent in the life cycle of a lake with no outlet—called "endorheic"—makes for an increasingly toxic environment. All but 18 percent of the world is made up of watersheds that eventually drain into the ocean. Endorheic watersheds drain into endorheic lakes, also known as sink lakes—as in the Salton Sink. Rain and snowmelt fill a sink, temporarily forming a lake until it dries up through seepage and evaporation, leaving salt pans, also called alkali flats—playas. Playas often contain high concentrations of inflow erosion products—minerals, pollutants, and salt that naturally leach into the rivers and streams feeding the sea.

Now, extreme salinity combined with high water temperatures in the Salton Sea provide an ideal breeding ground for the *clostridium botulinum* bacterium, which produces the *botulinum* neurotoxin and causes avian botulism. The bacterium grows in the millions of fish, which are consumed by hundreds of thousands of birds; the paralyzing neurotoxin kills the birds; and the maggots in the decomposing birds contract the disease and are then eaten by more fish and birds. Once the botulism reaches the maggot cycle, an outbreak spreads rapidly.

In the summer of 1996, U.S. Fish and Wildlife officers discovered fifty-eight dead and dying pelicans. A botulism outbreak was identified; from then on, hundreds a day were dying. Volunteers joined the officers to pull the newly dead bodies of the enormous waterfowl (as long as five feet with a nine-foot-plus wing span) from the water and off the shores so they could be incinerated before the maggots hatched. In the documentary *Plagues and Pleasures on the Salton Sea*, Clark Bloom, the manager of the refuge, recounted how the crematorium (the same model used for people) ran twenty-four hours a day and couldn't keep up. In four months, 14,000 birds died. Of that number, 10,000 were these enormous pelicans. Bloom sounded tired and depressed—determined to do what he could, but resigned to an inevitable habitat collapse.[1]

Every visionary new initiative around the Salton Sea seems to come with its boldly hyperbolic catchphrases, which persist even as reality is contradicting them. There are the classic originals: *the miracle of taming the desert* and *reclaiming the desert wasteland*. Later came the sexy gems like

---

1. *Plagues & Pleasures on the Salton Sea*. Tilapia Film, 2006.

The Glamour Capital of the Salton Sea, *The Queen of California's Vacation Empire*, and *The Jewel of the Salton Sea*. When it comes to positioning the Salton Sea as a wildlife sanctuary, it is no different. There's a new jewel on the block, according to certain scientists quoted on the Salton Sea Authority's website:[2] *The Crown Jewel of Avian Biodiversity*. I could never track down the particular scientists who were saying that.

MIKE AND I and my maimed Prius turned left onto Highway 111 and headed up the north side of the Salton Sea through the marginally inhabited blocks of Niland, then beyond the city limits and deeper into the desert to Salvation Mountain. In 1984, Leonard Knight, a wanderer and a prophet, stopped in the desert, like Abraham and Jacob before him, to build a monument to the Lord. On the bank of a dry riverbed, he mixed cement and paint and began to build his simple marker to proclaim to any who might find themselves on the eastern edge of the Colorado Desert, fifty miles from the nearest interstate on Beal Road, just this side of Slab City, this simple message: God Is Love.

Abraham set up his monument and then continued on to Egypt. Leonard stayed where he was and continued building. When cement became too expensive, he started using straw bales mixed with adobe. He used white and bright latex house paint to tell the world that God Is Love and God Loves You. Those words and hundreds of others wind around psychedelic flowers, birds, streams, hearts, and angels—*Bible Mark Matthew Luke John Jesus Love Jesus Fire*

---

2. Salton Sea Authority: http://saltonsea.ca.gov/. Accessed January 14, 2015. This description no longer appears on the website.

Jesus I Am A Sinner Come On To My Body And Into My Heart
Jesus Love GOD IS LOVE.

Over thirty years, Leonard built a mountain 50 feet tall and 150 feet across, using over 100,000 gallons of paint. And Leonard built more than a mountain; he built up so much goodwill that people started giving him gifts of paint, straw bales, and other materials he needed. People just started showing up with them, making an offering at the altar to love. Some looked around for a while and said thank you. Some stuck around to help.

Jon Krakauer's 1996 book, *Into the Wild*, tells the life story of Chris McCandless, who set out after college to live simply. He left his privileged family and path to law school, gave away his money, burned his IDs, and hit the road. Before walking into the Alaskan wilderness to live off the land, he spent time around the Salton Sea, staying for a while with a couple at Slab City. In the 2007 film version of the book directed by Sean Penn, Leonard Knight makes an appearance. Leonard gives McCandless and a girl he has met at the Slabs (played by Emile Hirsch and a pre-*Twilight* Kristen Stewart) a tour of his Salvation Mountain. In a beautiful blending of performance and reality or art and truth, the McCandless character looks up and around, clearly delighted and amazed. "Where'd you get the [materials]?" he asks Knight.

"Oh, a lot of people in the Valley just really love me," Knight replies with humility and sincerity. He is tall and lean, with weathered, sun-darkened skin and pure white hair, disheveled, with long bangs like a teenage boy's falling across his forehead. And he has that kind of energy and conviction. "I think the whole world is starting to love me, and I want to have the wisdom to love them back." He steps back, grins broadly, and kind of giggles, maybe at himself. "And that's about it, so . . ." He throws his fists up like an old-time strong man and pumps them quickly. "I really get excited."

The McCandless character asks, "So you really believe in love, then?"

Knight rocks forward, head cocked to one side, and his expression changes from wide grin and playful eyes to a look of absolute certainty and conviction. "Yeah." His eyes deepen, and he nods his head, coming down on certain words for emphasis. "And this is a love story that is staggering to everybody in the whole world, that *God really loves us*, a lot. *A lot*. Does that answer that?"

"Yeah." The McCandless character laughs a bit, nodding in response.

"Good," Knight says, his grin returning and his eyes brightening.

The film cuts to the three of them standing on the top of the mountain, looking down, then out over to the Slabs and beyond to the desert. "I really love it here," Knight says. "I think the freedom of this place is so beautiful to me. For me, I wouldn't move for ten million dollars. Unless I had to," he says with a chuckle. "So I am contented here in the desert, and I'm livin' where I wanna live, and I think good gets better."[3]

Being content in the desert at the Salton Sea and believing that *good gets better*—what an astonishing sentiment in a place whose history is one of profound discontent and big promises of *the best in the world* turning to ruin.

In their 130-year history, the Men of Renown have never

---

3. *Into the Wild*. Paramount Pictures, 2007.

been content to let the desert be what it is. Instead, they've tried endlessly to make it into something else, something that could benefit them, something that they could manipulate just enough to sell to someone, or promise to sell to someone, or sell the promise to someone.

Knight built something without trying to sell anything. He never asked for anything, never tried to get anyone to believe anything. He just made this monumental work of art to tell anyone who might be interested that God loves them. It might not reach to heaven. Maybe it can't be seen from outer space. But it's about the connection we all long for, about reaching up to God and reaching out to each other.

Leonard Knight died in February of 2014 at a care facility in El Cajon, California, just six blocks from the house my grandpa Webb built with his own hands, complete with the palm-tree fence posts.

MIKE AND I drive back through Niland and on to Highway 111, headed for a beach. Bombay Beach is about twenty miles north and west from Salvation Mountain and sits on the southern end of the San Andreas Fault, so when half of California breaks off and falls into the ocean, that's where it will start. Bombay Beach was presumably named to evoke an exotic, alluring foreign land like its neighboring cities of Mecca and Niland, which was meant to bring to mind the fertile, faraway Nile delta. But it also occurred to me on our way out of town that *nil* is Latin for nothing or zero.

Bombay Beach might have been christened after an exotic international city, but its developer, R. K. Gilligan, seems far less aspirational than other Salton Sea Men of Renown. He made no plans for yacht clubs or luxury hotels; he envisioned the place mostly as a trailer park. The city is nearly a perfect square pushed up to the edge of the sea, four blocks deep by eight blocks wide. There are no enticing theme-named streets here. It is left off Highway 111 onto Avenue A, then a quarter-mile to the city grid. Avenue A forms the north side of the square running all the way to 5th Street. Avenues are letters A through H; streets are numbers 1 through 5. It makes me wonder if Gilligan grew up in Manhattan, or had virtually no imagination. (As an explorer of fissures in narratives, I assure you that I doggedly researched, but could find no information on Gilligan's roots or the level of his creative faculties.) There is no paradise here, promised or otherwise.

But there exists one flourish, forming the south side of Bombay Beach's square—the Aisle of Palms. It's curious, at least to me, that a city has fourteen streets, and they all follow the grid system perfectly but one: the grand Aisle. What was Gilligan thinking? Maybe he was a stoic, practical engineer and land developer who did most of the job by the numbers (and letters). But as the layout for the city was nearly complete, he finally saw what was in front of him the whole time—his competent yet coy assistant. In the throes of love he reached for something more, and named that last avenue something grandly romantic.

Ironically, there are no palms anywhere on the Aisle of Palms, though I'm sure there were plans for them. What runs down the sea side of the Aisle of Palms is a seven-foot rammed-earth wall, a levee. The levee continues south along 5th Street all the way to Avenue A and then up the north side. The levee was built to protect Bombay Beach from the sea.

In 1976 and 1977, the years of the United States Bicentennial and the birth of punk rock, respectively, hurricanes Kathleen and Doreen made landfall on the northern Baja Peninsula in Mexico and crossed the border into Imperial County. Hurricane Kathleen brought record rainfall, which caused extensive flooding throughout the Colorado Desert, destroying hundreds of homes, causing three quarters of a billion dollars in agricultural damage, and drowning twenty-one people. Most of the destruction from Kathleen had not been repaired when Doreen hit twelve months later. Of course, all that water flooding the Colorado Desert from Mexicali to Palm Springs ended up in the Salton Sea. The sea level rose quickly, leaving half of Bombay Beach under water. The levee wall had been built around most of the city, but what was beyond the wall was abandoned.

When Mike and I park the Prius and scramble up the side of the levee wall to check out the water, it looks like some knuckleheads played a massive practical joke—they moved the sea. It no longer laps at the levee or threatens the city; in fact, it looks like it's running from it. Since the catastrophic floods of forty years ago, the sea has slowly been retreating, first back to its historic level and then below it. In the last decade, its evaporation picked up speed due to a decrease in agricultural runoff and the long and ongoing California drought.

After the one-two punch from Kathleen and Doreen, the Men of Renown, the California Riviera dream developers and hucksters packed up their filmstrips and pamphlets, discontinued the sales junkets from Los Angeles and San Diego, and left town. Bombay Beach cut its losses and gave up the trailer homes beyond the wall to the elements. As the water receded, the abandoned trailers sank down into the muddy earth. These old Airstream and D.I.Y. trailers were soaked in the corrosive salt from the sea, scorched by the limitless sun, and baked by the relentless heat. The paint bleached and released its bonds; the aluminum and plywood sheeting peeled back to give the elements access to their insides and structural skeletons.

Almost all of those trailers and other ruins beyond the wall are gone now. Even the mud is gone, leaving just the dry, alkaline seabed. So the last local industry of Bombay Beach is almost gone—its decay. Pompeii was preserved by volcanic ash, the Great Wall of China has been repaired and rebuilt repeatedly—but the marginal construction of a vacation-paradise trailer park in one of the planet's uber-extreme climates has a much shorter life expectancy. Not that the decay was much of an income-generating industry, but it did attract more attention from the post-apocalyptic-ruin-porn-eco-disaster-tourists than other Salton Sea destinations. I think it's the trailers. For most of urban consumer-culture America, a brand-new trailer would signify hard times—so the ancient ruins of an entire trailer park seem like the remains of a strange and other people.

Bombay Beach has been the subject of many magazine and newspaper articles, blogs, YouTube videos, television episodes, and a handful of documentary films. They almost all use some combination of the words *ruined, ruins, failed, post-apocalyptic, abandoned, ghost town, world's end, godforsaken*—and on and on in that vein. The same images are repeatedly shown, the seemingly poignant meaning discovered by the explorer and his inner artist (or inner theologian, humanitarian, or niche historian). He sees something beautiful in the garbage of this discarded city, and he's drawn to capture the otherworldliness of it, to film or photograph it. And so many people's "inner artist" draws them to capture the same images: the "Welcome to Bombay Beach" sign, the decaying trailers, the smashed 1970s television, the decapitated armchair sitting in the shallow sea water at a meaningful angle, the floating and rotting dead fish. Before noticing this phenomenon, I had already taken exactly the same shots.

On his Strange Geographies website, Ransom Riggs calls it "the most famously depressing place on earth."[4] Abandoned USA, a project developed to document abandoned buildings and cities across America, says of Bombay Beach, "Once a glorious resort town, very little remains at this desolate spot by the sea. The water smells of petrol and dead fish, and the water shines an almost fluorescent red."[5] The thing is—it's not abandoned. People do live here—families, retirees, regular kinds of people—just not that many of them. About three hundred people call it home.

It must be hard to live in a place where most tourists visit just to see how desiccated everything is. I wonder what it's like for a resident couple to see their trailer, their home, on a website or on YouTube as an example of post-apocalyptic ruin? Do they feel ashamed? Angry? Or do they feel some of that dark pride, happy to be noticed at all?

---

4. Ransom Riggs, "The Accidental Sea," Mentalfloss.com. May 12, 2011. http://mentalfloss.com/article/27722/strange-geographies-accidental-sea. Accessed January 14, 2015.

5. Abandoned USA, "Salton City, CA: Salton Sea, Part I." http://abandonedusa.com/site/bombai-beach-ca-salton-sea-part-1. Accessed January 13, 2015. This site is currently offline.

It must be hard not to think that the world is trying to kill you when everything around you is dying. Mike and I walk down to the edge of the water, where thousands of dead fish line the beach. There are rotting bird carcasses, decaying cars, trailer homes, and buildings long dead. If you stay here long enough, even just an hour, the heat dries your skin to a chalky smoothness, loose and wrinkled. The blanching glare gets in behind your eyes, and the stench coming off the sea penetrates your hair. And when you look around at all the stuff used for living everyday life—the remains of houses, refrigerators, washing machines, clothes, beds, bikes, and toys—strewn everywhere, picked over and ruined, the artist in you leaves, and things just seem broken and sad.

WHEN WE GET BACK to the car, it is covered with a layer of the Salton Sea's future. I sit in the driver's seat and look through the toxic film on the front windshield. I click the wiper switch on and twist it forward to spray the washing fluid, hold it to get a good soak, then release it. The wipers first smear a mud veneer, and then, after another twist and spray, the wipers squeak the windshield clean, two shiny, raised eyebrows cut out of the dust-covered car. I imagine the salt and toxins beginning to eat away at the finish of the paint job. My first thought is *I need a carwash*.

Then I twist the wiper switch to turn on the rear wiper and spray the back window. I look in the rearview mirror and see fluid running down the window, cutting channels through the dust, while the stump of the wiper arm waves back and forth, impotent, embarrassed, apologetic.

Back on Highway 111, Mike and I ride silently along the shoreline to the northern tip of the Salton Sea, to Mecca, where we cut over to Highway 86 and aim the Prius down the western shore. I point out Travertine Rock, a fifty-foot out-cropping where the high-water mark from the ancient lake can be seen at forty feet above sea level. We explore Desert Shores, where the developers had carved up the shoreline into ten long fingers jutting out into the sea. Homes have either come and gone or never materialized. There are a half-dozen lots occupied on Capri Road, one on Marseille Lane, three on Naples, and two on Venice. Honolulu and Acapulco Lanes, as well as the four other upscale fingers, are entirely vacant.

And finally we approach Salton City, the crown jewel if not the most ambitious of the California Riviera developments, where just two days ago *The Salton Sea: Yesterday and Today* was semi-surreptitiously slid across the library counter to my eager hands—Salton City, where Mike and I were chased from the shore and back into the Prius by that cadaverous stench.

Two days. Two days ago we might have assumed that soul-stinging smell was simply from thousands of rotting fish. Now we know the complicated truth. It begins with numerous tons of algae blooms sent into a state of hyper-reproduction by the endless supply of nitrogen and phospho-rus from agricultural runoff, which, because of the extreme heat or strangling salinity levels, die and sink peacefully to the sea floor. There, through a lovely cycle-of-life process, they are decomposed by bacteria, which, because of the over-abundance of algae, multiply to levels so preposterous that they use up all the oxygen in the water around them. At this point, shifting currents send the hypoxic death zone through the sea, asphyxiating tens of thousands of fish as it moves, eventually, to the surface, where it releases that infamous noxious odor—with probably some rotting fish smell mixed in as a final flourish.

We turn onto S. Marina Drive, through the "Welcome to Salton City" signs straddling the broad main thoroughfare, this time not bothering to stop at the Salton Community Services District building, a strip of storefronts that's home to not only local governing types, American Dreams Real Estate, and Mancuts, but also the aforementioned Salton City branch of the Imperial County Library.

We follow the grand curve of S. Marina Drive that Albert Frey laid out more than fifty years ago, past the cul-de-sacs and curlicues of Lanes, Circles, Avenues, and Courts, not one of which is a through way; most don't run for more than a block uninterrupted. We turn onto one and follow it around, getting back on to S. Marina Drive, then onto another, always coming back to S. Marina. I let the Prius take us where it will.

It doesn't matter where we go. Street after Avenue after Circle, Court, and Drive are all the same—empty. Sea Life Avenue and Shore Maze Street, Sea Dream and Rainbow Drive, Sea Way and Sea Air Circle. Street after empty street, lot after empty lot. Of the more than 20,000 lots laid out in 1965, only 516 have ever been developed. There are no reliable figures on how many have actually been sold. Some have been sold multiple times by the developer; others have been resold again and again as buyer after buyer gets talked into an investment opportunity, sobers up, and then starts looking for someone to take it off their hands.

Court records from 1977 show that 2,190 property owners tried to get their money back from M. Penn Phillips, the original developer. A summary of the suit for the appellate court says, "Generally speaking the complaint alleged a classic land sale fraud operation. A veritable catalogue of alleged misrepresentations, stated to be part of a 'canned sales pitch' made to all purchasers, is presented; and it is alleged that defendants knew these misrepresentations to be such, and that the members of the Association reasonably relied thereon to their detriment."[6]

By that time, all the Men of Renown had moved on—some to new opportunities, others to a state where they weren't barred from doing business. And in the case of Ray Ryan, the Desert Shores developer—he was taken out by a car bomb around the same time as the court decision against M. Penn Phillips in 1977. Sometimes dreams die. Sometimes they blow up in your face.

WHATEVER THE CASE, the dream of the Salton Sea Riviera was no longer being pitched. It had moved from possibility to nostalgia. Every mention of the Salton Sea now comes with prefaces like "Once a glamorous vacation paradise" or "Formerly a playground for the jet set." There is regular mention of visits from Frank Sinatra, Jerry Lewis, and the Beach Boys. I have my doubts. What were they doing down here? Swinging? Playing on the playground?

How is it that a dream of a future that never materialized can become a longed-for past? Emotionally, desiring something in the future and desiring something in the past are nearly the same movement. It's probably harder to sell

6. *Salton City Etc. Owners Assn. v. M. Penn Phillips Co.* Civ. No. 50488. Court of Appeals of California, Second Appellate District, Division One. November 18, 1977.

a vision of the past than a vision of the future. The past comes with reality, with ruins. The future has brochures and PowerPoint presentations and promises. Empires are built on the promises of the future.

I prefer the ruins.

I'm not interested in empires unless they have fallen or are stumbling, tripping forward and about to fall. From the crumbling incompleteness of the Great Wall to the burned-out shell of Bombay Beach.

I like broken things. I'm not overly impressed by grandeur, opulence, or structural marvel. I'm drawn to rubble, ruin, and collapse. I've been this way as long as I can remember.

I remember, in first grade, walking with Mike down Ventura Boulevard in Ventura, California. We were in a neighborhood I heard my grandmother describe as *run-down*, a neighborhood where I spent the first eight years of my life, and we were looking around at all the buildings, the businesses, the structures, and thinking that they all looked like they used to be something else, like better or cleaner—or open. We decided to explore a closed, abandoned gas station.

It was a classic old building, a Streamline Moderne gas station, with the awning built out over the pumps, two service bays, and the angled, air-traffic-control-tower glass office. It had clearly seen better days. The roll-up doors on the service bays were gone, and we went inside and looked down into the wells. There were no lifts—there were concrete stairs going down into these wells, so the mechanics could get under the cars to work on them. There were workbenches and an old refrigerator on its side. Everything was greasy and messy and damaged; the metal door to the office was bent and rusty.

Then these big kids saw us and swaggered into the building and said we couldn't be there, and one of them picked up a pipe, so we ran. I remember it being really scary and intensely compelling at the same time.

When my family would drive past that old gas station, I would imagine what it would have been like when it was gleaming and new. When it first opened, shiny cars would have pulled up, and uniformed attendants would have come out to "Fill 'er up." For me, no such romantic vision attaches itself to a new gas station.

I wonder if my attraction to abandoned and broken-down buildings is simply the result of my circumstances, living in that neighborhood for several years and then moving and growing up in the city I did. Saint Paul is a city that used to be. I guess another way of saying that is that it has a sense of history. Either way, there's a lot of looking back. Back to the days when James J. Hill built the Great Northern Railway and Saint Paul was the most important city west of Chicago. Back to the days when F. Scott Fitzgerald sat in a third-floor apartment on Summit Avenue and wrote his first novel after dropping out of Princeton. Back to the days when gangsters filled the city and it was glamourous and dangerous. I like the stories, but I like the structures better. The broken-down buildings mark what used to be.

Broken things, the ruins of something once great or mundane, are pure possibility, because they contain the potential for absolute redemption. When I see a structure being restored, every staircase or window that is repaired or replaced limits the building's possibilities. Every decision that's made rules out every other decision that could have been made. Until finally the structure stands as a very narrow glimpse of one person's understanding of what redemption looks like. All possibility removed.

Brokenness seems more true than greatness. And I trust brokenness more than the promises of greatness. When has greatness ever helped anyone out? Are people's lives profoundly changed when they finally realize how great they are, when they come to accept and love the greatness in themselves?

I don't trust that I know what actual redemption looks like. But I do know what the *potential* for redemption looks like.

S. Marina Drive and Sea Kist, Redondo and Sea Raider, Sea Nymph and S. Marina, S. Marina and Yacht Club Place.

Yacht Club Place is a broad parkway, two generous lanes running in each direction, with a wide median down the center. Once it was landscaped lavishly. Now the stubs of long-dead palm trees stick out like giant cigarette butts stabbed into the sand in relatively regular intervals along the three blocks to the sea.

As Mike and I drive along, the asphalt roadbed crumbles under the weight of the Prius's tires until it mingles unrecognizably with the desert dirt at the spot where the Salton Bay Yacht Club once stood. There are no recognizable ruins remaining. Mike and I walk down along what may have been the marina. The smell isn't as bad as it has been. There's a breeze, and out on the water, on a spit or a jetty, there are hundreds of brown pelicans. When they fly, they look prehistoric—enormous and gorgeous and immune to extinction.

I'm just about done forming a reflection on nature's ability to impose beauty in the context of man's ugliness, or something like that, when Mike says, "This isn't sand."

"What?"

"This isn't sand we're standing on. It's fish bones."

I look down. It's true. I crouch down and scoop some up in my hand and see everything from bleached bone as small as sand grains to recognizable vertebrae and fin fragments. When I look up, along the shoreline, the fishbone beach stretches beyond my view. There are ribbons of different-size bones, from whole heads and intact backbones, to twig- and matchbook-size sections of ribcage and tailfin, to the finely chopped, to the tiny grains. And then the ribbons repeat again, several more times. If I was some kind of biologist/geologist, I could date each major fish die-off and calculate the rate of breakdown from "washed up on the shore with a million and a half of his buddies" to "bleached white bone beach sand." But as a niche historian, I can only sit back heavily and feel overwhelmed. This is a long way from an engineering miscalculation more than a century ago—and this is before things are going to get really bad.

Mike reads my face or feels what I feel across our Irish twin-brother bond. He strolls over and reaches down his hand. "Come on." He pulls me up and points us to the Prius. I slowly unclench my hand as we walk, letting the fishbone sand return to the earth.

Back inside our capsule, the bracing air conditioning brightens the mood. I turn the music back on for the first time since Niland. Slade is playing "Run, Run Away" on the mix tape. Mike and I loved this song the first time we heard it, riding around in another car, back in Saint Paul, several decades ago. Of course it's super-catchy, with the guitar hook and the vocal doubling it, but it was the refrain that cracked us up—*See chameleon, lying there in the sun, all things to everyone, run, run away.* We thought the line *all things to everyone* was so funny; it had a whimsical generosity that appealed to us. We started using it with our family and friends to resolve disputes. When things were tense or someone had wronged someone else, when things were at a standstill, one of us would proclaim "All things to everyone " and we could move on, say sorry, pull each other close. Basically it meant, Who knows who's right or wrong? We all want the best for everyone.

As we got older, we talked about it as a sort of existential blessing. See the chameleon lying there in the sun. Is it sunning itself? Is it dead? Whatever—*all things to everyone!* We all receive the gifts of this life—embodiment, breath, the ability to love—and we all receive its sorrow. *All things to everyone* is both a blessing and a statement of reality. With Mike and I both singing almost unselfconsciously, I make a U-turn and head back down Yacht Club Drive to S. Marina.

I take a right. It is here that we encounter a mistake made almost seven decades ago by Albert Frey or M. Penn Phillips or some other Men of Renown, the possible irony of which they would never have paused to consider. Yacht Club Drive is apparently the dividing line in Salton City. Like the Main Street designator, everything below it is south, and everything above it is north. So while we headed south along S. Marina Drive on its swoop from Highway 86 to the beach where the Salton Bay Yacht Club once stood (and the beach used to be made of sand), now that we're on the swoop back around toward Highway 86, everything is designated north. But while the city planners used capital S for south, as in S. Marina Drive, they didn't use capital N for north. They used the abbreviation No instead. So, North Marina Drive is written on the street sign as No Marina Drive. I turn off the music.

We drive past No Sea Life, No Sea Dream, No Sea Elf, No Sea King, No Sea Queen, No Sea Prince, No Sea Nymph, Urchin, or View. At the corner of No Marina Drive and No Riviera, I take a right. Now I'm driving on near-desert floor, because the asphalt roads here have completely deteriorated. I take my foot off the accelerator pedal and let the Prius move us forward at idle speed.

Finally I see the street sign and put my foot on the brake, turn the engine off, and get out of the car. The intersection of No Riviera and No Empire. I walk to the street sign and grasp it at shoulder height to steady myself.

"Let's call this it," I proclaim to Mike. "Grandpa's lot. Grandpa's land. This is our land. This is the place he picked on the map and put his money on."

I look up.

I wonder. And then, as I did on the Great Wall of China, I wave. But here, now, I wave vigorously, gratefully.

I ADMIT IT—I'M afraid of a lot of things. Mostly people— saying bad things about me, or not giving me a loan, or re-plying, "Well, you should have thought about that before."

And most of the time I'm afraid to die. I'm also afraid when I think of the endlessness of the universe. Have you ever felt that way? Where you start thinking about the earth and all the other planets in our solar system, and how our solar system is inside the galaxy, and how our galaxy and all other galaxies are inside the universe—and the universe is inside of . . . what? It's inside of nothing. It just keeps going on forever. But how can something be contained by nothing? How can there be no end?

And have you ever thought about being in outer space? What if you were in space, and you had to do a space walk to fix the space station, and then your tether broke and you just floated away? Would you keep floating away until you ran out of air? Or even then, would your body just keep floating off forever—literally never stopping?

That really freaks me out. And then it makes me wonder about when Jesus ascended into heaven, when the disciples watched him disappear into the clouds. Where did he go? And where is he? Because I don't believe heaven is up—like it's a physical place you could get to. So did Jesus just keep going up and up and into space? Is that where he is?

It makes me think that my one hope is that if I ever have to take a space walk and my tether breaks and I float away forever—that I might float by Jesus.

But I would already be so beyond scared—and then if I saw another person floating toward me, it might just be too much. And how would I know it was Jesus? I don't know what Jesus looks like—unless he looks like those Sunday-school pictures with the robe and the beard and the long hair. But still, that could be anyone. Everyone looked like that back then. It's not like I would recognize his face. And it would be even more terrifying to see someone floating toward me without a spacesuit on. But where would he get a spacesuit? They didn't have them back then.

I would for sure think he was an alien. Even if he looked like Sunday-school Jesus. So I think I would try to float myself in the opposite direction if an alien Jesus came toward me.

But maybe I wouldn't be able to get away. Changing direction in space is probably pretty hard. So maybe alien spaceman Jesus catches up with me. And he takes my hand, and he looks at me, and maybe in a reading-my-thoughts kind of way he says, "Have a look. What can you see from outer space?"

I look down. First I see the Prius. I see Mike shading his eyes, leaning against it and smoking. I see me holding on to the street sign: No Riviera and No Empire. Jesus laughs. "Look around," he says.

I look down again, and I see the Great Wall of China snaking its way around through history. I see Douglas Coupland on that field at the end of his book. I see Shenzhen and the statue of Deng Xiaoping. I see the towers of Shanghai. And I see my grandpa's shed, and his palm-tree fence, and the millions of tilapia gasping for breath. I see Salvation Mountain and Leonard Knight blessing me, and I see the Perfect Carwash.

And then I see me. Standing at the intersection of No Empire and No Riviera.